ODHAMS

READING MATTER FOR
A SOCIETY ON
A JOURNEY

By

Colin Bearne

Design & Production - Jaki Porter

Dedicated to my grandfather
Ted Child
and those who worked with him.

CONTENTS

Odhams architect designed
and listed water tower
at the North Watford
works site.

PREFACE

There are a number of factors, largely interrelated, attracting me to write this survey. The main one is that there was a family connection with Odhams through my maternal grandfather. This was one of the reasons which led to me spending my formative years in Watford, the town which saw the full flourishing and the final sad demise of the firm. Not surprisingly most of the many books in our household came from Odhams. I have, over the years since childhood, amassed a collection of more than 400 of these titles. Odhams became, in its heyday, one of the country's major book, newspaper and periodical producers, at the cutting edge of printing and photogravure technology. The output of so many books from such a source is very much worth close study. As I view them again I am trying to provide an assessment of the firm's book output, as far as I know something never attempted before.

The history of Odhams Press has been presented to the public twice. On the first occasion when one of the family – W.B.Odhams – covered the period from roughly 1840 to the year he retired from the management – 1935. Basically this is an autobiography, and as such has unfortunately little to do with books and deals at length with newspapers and illustrated magazines. It also has to do with personalities, notably the man who became the guiding spirit of the firm – Julius Salter Elias. The latter's biography, published under the title Viscount Southwood – in his later years Elias had been elevated to the peerage – covers the period up to his death in 1946 and begins with his first association with the firm. It, also, has little to say about book production and deals in the main with newspapers and magazines.

What can now be viewed as the house's declining years up to the 1970s and the various amalgamations and take-overs, have been given general treatment, but never been chronicled in detail.

In the absence of informative archive material I am making general judgements, based on just the books themselves, which may in the end be the right thing to do.

**Odhams
North Watford works.**
Top - 1935
Bottom - circa 1953

BEGINNINGS AND DEVELOPMENT

In 1847 William Odhams, a compositor working on the **Morning Post,** founded a firm bearing his own name. He had originally come from Sherborne, Dorset. The firm was based not far from the **Post** in the Savoy area of London. The business began with contracts for a number of small circulation specialist newspapers such as the **Investors' Guardian** and the **County Council Times**.

In 1892, by which time the portfolio of largely trade newspapers had grown considerably, William Odhams sold the business to his sons, but continued to take an unwelcome part in its running, to such an extent that the brothers broke away and set up their own business – Odhams Brothers Ltd. Eventually, in 1898, the two firms were amalgamated to form Odhams Ltd. Julius Elias had only joined the firm in 1894, as a clerk and glorified office boy. He now became a director of the new business, and was due to become its guiding spirit until his death in 1946.

In the period between 1849 and the end of the First World War Odhams output of actual books, as opposed to newspapers and journals, was very slight, less than three a year. It was only at the start of the 1920s that the annual number of titles began to increase to more than half a dozen. By then previous forays into classic fiction included Edgar Allan Poe and H.G. Wells and biographies, notably of Horatio Bottomley, with whom Odhams were later to be involved in a protracted legal dispute. Bottomley, whose often outrageous behaviour caused a furore in his own age, is now largely forgotten by our own, even in the world of publishing. Unfortunately for Odhams Bottomley was not the only such figure with whom the firm

was to come into contact. At least in Bottomley's case the firm ended up with a successful magazine –**John Bull**. Thus, apart from the occasional book, it would be fair to say that magazines and newspapers occupied the greater part of Odhams early production and effort. The papers were significant national ones – **The People** and **Reynolds News**, and, from the point of view of books, the most significant was the **Daily Herald**. In the developing bitter war for increased circulation figures, with targets of first 2 million and then 3 million, the **Herald's** main rival was Beaverbrook's **Daily Express**. It happened, perhaps predictably, that the political tendencies of the **Express** ran counter to those of the **Herald** (organ of the Labour movement), yet both, in news terms, were competing for the same upwardly mobile middle-class and blue-collar worker readership, and that is where Odhams connection with the mass production of books really starts.

Before turning to the subject of our main concern it might be as well to examine in some detail what we can discover about possible policy-forming trends in the conduct of the firm in the early 1930s. By comparison with the 1920s this decade is often viewed in retrospect as being drab, grim and somewhat depressing with its economic and political uncertainties, but from the point of view of the mass-media (including cinema, radio, and the newly emerging television which were to have a massive impact on book-publishing – both positive and negative) the decade proved to be extremely exciting.

In 1935, the year in which W.B.Odhams' biographical account comes to and end, the firm was settled in Long Acre, WC2 and although its own printing facilities were also situated in and around Fleet Street it had already begun to contract out certain jobs to other printers in London and in the provinces. In this respect there was a particular attraction to what might be called the 'Chiltern Corridor', with its ready supply of paper from firms such as John Dickinsons, and its healthy base of provincial printers. The town of Watford, with its easy access from London by road (partly via the newly constructed North Orbital) and rail, was particularly attractive, and the following two years saw the emergence of Odhams' long-term relationship with the town. Watford's situation on a north-south main line, and its nearness to the A1 and A4 eased the question of distribution to all areas of the country. Having already acquired premises in Manchester to facilitate magazine and newspaper distribution in the north, in 1935 Odhams acquired a 16 acre site in North Watford bounded by the North Orbital, the A412 and a branch of the London Midland and Scottish Railway. It was to be a base from which a steady stream of papers, magazines and books would appear for more than thirty years. The plant was also the UK's major base for the new process of photogravure. This was the result of an initiative begun by Elias Salter, who, in practical terms, stood at the head of Odhams in 1935, was an unusual figure amongst his peers. Born into a relatively poor family of seven children, he had little or no formal education and certainly hardly any training in either the press or printing. His father was a small-time dealer at what we might now call the market-trader level. His only early contact with the business was the time he had spent as a newspaper delivery boy! There can be little doubt that he became an autodidact of the kind at whom many of Odhams later books were aimed. By dint of hard work and the exercise of business acumen, Elias had risen 'through the ranks' until, by 1934, he was instrumental in taking the firm forwards into the world of illustrated magazines and the London dailies and the fierce competition which had arisen between them.

Readership was expanding and a newly literate generation was already an avid consumer of news, gossip, scandal, crime and romance and also - sport. This was a great decade for Association football and cricket. Attendances at all sporting events were phenomenal – and growing yearly. People desperately wanted to read about sport, and everybody, but everybody who could, danced. There was an additional fascination with speed – the Schneider Trophy, Brooklands, and the Isle of Man TT races. Technological advances were being made everywhere, and widely publicised. The face of Britain was changing almost without anyone being aware. Our concentration on the fraught international crises of the period – the triumphant march of fascism, the Spanish Civil War, the emergence of the Soviet Union as a twentieth century world power, and international conflicts in Abyssinia, China and Manchuria – all were counterbalanced by a desperate inward-looking desire for rush, noise and fun. Also the population of Britain was becoming increasingly urban and suburban, increasingly literate and, within certain limits, increasingly sophisticated and affluent.

This was the kind of readership that Elias knew bought the now extremely popular weekly magazines such as *John Bull* which, after much legal wrangling and financial negotiation, had recently become an Odhams title. In the late 20's and early 30's the national dailies had been absorbed into conglomerates, which owned both daily and weekly papers, and also weekly magazines. The Odhams 'group' included *Illustrated*, *Picturegoer,* various other magazines, *The People*, and most importantly from the book point of view, the *Daily Herald*. This was the Labour Party's official organ which had got into financial trouble, had a falling circulation, and in which a majority share had been acquired by Odhams. Since Elias's views were as far as known not markedly left-wing this could have proved an uncomfortable situation, yet it was one which continued with various ups and downs until the **Herald** itself went under in the 1960s, under pressure from other dailies, TV, and possibly popular disenchantment with politically committed journalism.

Both the **Express** and the **Herald** offered gifts to their subscribers as part of their marketing campaigns. These gifts covered a wide range of personal items and household goods. At a time when total family incomes in the social groups concerned were still fairly restricted these offers no doubt generated a significant increase in circulations. From the point of view of the present study the introduction of *books* as gifts is of primary interest. The books appear to have been offered in return for the accumulation by readers of a certain number of book coupons. This meant that a reasonable number of books could be 'collected' at a much lower price than at conventional bookshops, then the only other retail outlet. Trouble with the Publishers' Association and the Net Book Agreement was initially avoided by the offer of 'classics', In other words long pre-published titles. In Odhams case these were available in two forms, either red or blue boards, or a dark brown morocco binding. The first series to appear in this way was a 16 volume set of Dickens. The choice of this author is interesting at this particular time and given the kind of readership at which the books were aimed. Dickens' popularity in appeal and popularness in content was at the time unchallenged. Characters from his novels had gone into metaphor and folk-culture, his works were serialised in magazines and on the newly burgeoning wireless. Adapted excerpts were acted by both amateur and professional companies. Apart from anything else, staff in the Odhams book department would have grown up with Dickens as an icon, whose sometimes humorous, sometimes bitter critique of Victorian England and its social policies was in tune with the increasing support in the 1930s for state intervention. No doubt those who had collected all 16 volumes felt they had something worth gracing their sitting-room bookshelf.

After Dickens came a number of almost predictable authors Trollope, Fielding, Blackmoor (Lorna Doone), Sewell (Black Beauty), George Eliot, Thackeray, Dumas and many others – all in the recognisable bindings that had enclosed the Dickens. Matters became slightly more problematic where living authors were concerned, such as Wells and Shaw, particularly the latter. In the decade concerned these two were celebrities, as we would call them – in the sense that interviews they gave, especially on international affairs or moral matters were widely reported in the daily and weekly press. As it happened their views were not out of tune with those of the **Herald**. In Shaw's case in particular considerable controversy arose between Odhams and his original publishers who were selling at a price significantly higher than that paid by readers of the **Herald**. The argument became increasingly bitter until eventually brought to an end by Shaw himself. It seemed as though if the author himself had no objection to his works being, as Odhams opponents put it, 'virtually given away' then there was little that could be done. Thus, while there was an obvious commercial motive behind the book coupon scheme, there was also the non-economic analysis that this was an effective way of ensuring that more and more people, from a widening section of society, had access to 'good' literature. It goes without saying that a single volume complete Shakespeare also became available in the years after 1935.

As with many Odhams books, these 'classics' now frequently find their way to second-hand bookshops, jumble sales and boot fairs. Many are in good condition, suffering, if at all, from weathering rather than intensive reading. This leads one to question both motives for buying, and for selling, or at least to reassess them. Often the books seem to have been acquired for prestige reasons – to be seen as much as to be read, though here I may risk being overly cynical.

As the second half of the '30s progressed the motive and the emphasis seemed to change. Now it was not the 'classics', but the goal of 'self-improvement' which achieved prominence. Accumulation of a 'set' of books was still the vehicle for this self-education or self-improvement. The 'books' in question formed part of a series entitled **Live Successfully** (1938). These publications would be better described as pamphlets. They seldom exceeded 70 pages. Volume one was subtitled 'How to discover the real you', and volume ten 'How to develop your personality' - the pamphlets in fact covered a wide range of moral, social and psychological issues, and they reflected a growing post-Freudian interest in how and why we behave as we do. What we no longer have, if indeed it ever existed, is a breakdown of who ordered what! But since we lack any elaboration of the target audience such fascinating questions must remain unanswered. In fact, as in general with Odhams, we can only speculate on publishing policy in the light of what actually appeared.

Concurrently with the classics since 1935-6 Odhams had been, in common with other major publishers, putting out a range of what are usually referred to as reference titles. **The New Standard Encyclopedia and World Atlas** in fact dated as far back as 1932 (with an introduction by the headmaster of Eton!). Dictionaries and separately published atlases fell into the same mould. Odhams productions of this kind were cheaply but smartly turned out on the basis that no

household should be without one, and many have stood the test of time, despite the dated nature of some of their contents. In various formats, single or multi-volume, Odhams went on publishing encyclopedias for almost thirty years, but the large compendia, with titles such as **Universal Knowledge A to Z** and **Everybody's Book of Facts**, produced mostly at the firm's new Watford plant, flourished in 1938-9, the uncertain years leading up to the Second World War. 'Everybody's' as a title wording seemed to encapsulate both the wider sales and the need to spread knowledge as widely as possible. One symptom of the times was the appearance of **Everybody's Book of Politics**, the anonymous editor of which writes in the preface:

> *"It is a strange world that we live in today – a world racked by depression, and tortured by wars and rumours of wars; yet a world heavy with the promise of an unfulfilled peace and plenty for all. Abroad dictatorships spring up, accompanied by suspicions, threats and jealousies. At home, there is uneasiness and dissatisfaction with the poverty and sickness, pain, unhappiness and unemployment that afflict so many. Democracy – it may be civilisation itself – is threatened.*
>
> *Yet if we live today in conditions that we deplore, it is to some extent our own fault…*
>
> *… this book is offered in the belief that it will help to clarify many issues and enable citizens of this country to frame their opinions in the light of considered and mature knowledge with all the available and relevant information before them."*

Such was the intention! It would be fascinating to discover the identity of some of Odhams anonymous authors. We know only that the historian Harold Wheeler edited a number of informational texts.

Books such as this were plainly but smartly presented in dark blue or dark red boards on quite coarse but durable paper, and with a conventional font and font size. *The Book of Politics* was one of the publications of these years to bear on the title page the Mayflower galleon logo which had become an identifying feature of numbers of Odhams books. There had been other logos – the firm had used a globe and rays logo, and also a head of Minerva. With the development of coloured front and end-papers these various logos were often combined in a fanciful design.

Methods of sale also seem to have changed slightly. Instead of coupon collecting regular readers of the

papers and illustrated magazines could now avail themselves of the opportunity of acquiring books at a 'special' price, presumably lower than that at which they were on sale at normal book-sellers. Of these the only one advertised in any of the Odhams publications was W H Smiths. Two representative advertisements are given here –

As we shall see later, book clubs also came to play a significant role in fiction sales.

Book marketing through Odhams own publications

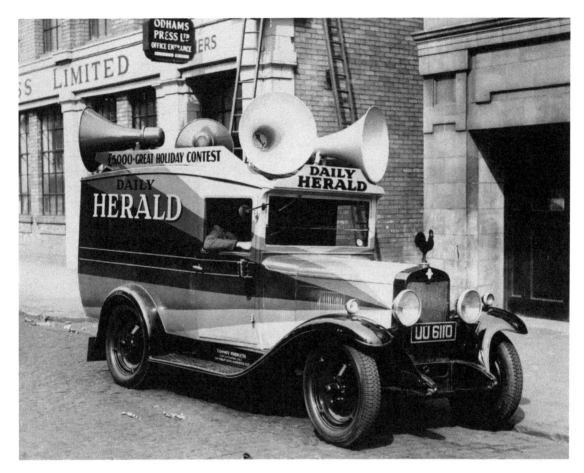

Fighting the subscription
wars, circa 1938.

PRINTING

To begin with some books seem to have been printed, together with newspapers and magazines, at the firm's London plant at Long Acre off Fleet Street. Presumably, when these premises were destroyed in the wartime bombing (January, 1918) other firms helped out for a period, and some printing was contracted out. As early as 1935, however, printing was done by the firm of Greycaines in Watford. In fact they were responsible for printing a considerable number of Odhams titles over a lengthy period. The successful relationship with this Watford firm must surely have been another factor influencing Odhams' decision to site their new plant on a 16-acre site in the town. Two other Watford firms were later contributors to the production of Odhams books, Fishburn Printing Inks, and, more importantly, Sun Engraving Ltd. Some of the later specialist titles *100 of the World's Best Photographs* (1939), for example, were produced entirely at Sun Engraving, using the firm's photogravure process. In their day the Sun and Odhams dominated the Watford industrial scene, until their merger and closure by Robert Maxwell.

My maternal grandfather, who worked both at Long Acre and the offices in the Watford plant, would take me as a small child into town on a Saturday 'shopping', and I remember waiting, more or less patiently, while he chatted to work colleagues and acquaintances, he being offered and accepting, as was the custom with print workers, pinches of snuff.

Another long-term Odhams relationship was with the firm of Tinlings of Prescot in Liverpool, not all that distant from Odhams northern office in Manchester.

Although from 1937-1947 the majority of titles were printed in Watford, some work was contracted out to regional centres as dispersed as Tonbridge, Norwich and Edinburgh, while a small number were produced at the top of the 'Chiltern Corridor', by Hazell, Watson and Viney in Aylesbury. There were, presumably, very particular strategic factors which made it desirable to print out of house, war damage and specialist needs have been mentioned already, but there were also obviously times when Watford was operating at full capacity, especially during the war years. Under these circumstances, when plant was busy for example with the printing of Ministry of Information and Home Office leaflets and pamphlets, some later titles were contracted out to well-known printers such as the redoubtable Clays of Bungay, Suffolk. On rare occasions, with maybe two or three titles, printing post-war was undertaken outside the UK, in Holland, for example.

Odhams relationship with its sizeable Watford neighbour Sun Engraving and Printing was interesting. Even before the Second World War the Sun had undertaken gravure work for Odhams' illustrated magazines and Elias had at one stage tried to buy the firm. The Sun rejected the offer but went on to print some few, mostly art, books for Odhams. Ironically Odhams found itself bedfellow with the Sun when both firms were absorbed into IPC Magazines in the 1970s.

Odhams economic contribution to the trade of book-making was thus of some significance during the firm's heyday.

LULWORTH COVE, DORSET

Examples of artwork from
the 1950s and 1960s

ARTWORK

The titles of a large proportion of Odhams books contain the word 'illustrated' or the phrase 'in pictures', and it is true to say now, over half a century after the collapse of Odhams as an independent entity, that the public perception of the firm, fuelled partly by awareness of Odhams portfolio of illustrated magazines, is as a source of picture books. Rare indeed was the non-fiction book which did not have some kind of images, either to demonstrate a procedure, or to illustrate an object being referred to in the text. As the 1930s progressed the overwhelming majority of books appearing was of this kind. Even the early encyclopaedic volumes had line drawings.

The originals of these line drawings presumably remained with the artist or were stored somewhere in Odhams' London offices in Long Acre, but this situation was to change with the introduction of a much higher proportion of photographic illustrations. To start with, as in the case of *The Silver Jubilee Book*, the photographic illustrations were predominantly from archive or agency sources and thus presumably the problem of production and storage of the images was not great. As time went by, however, and the 1930s passed into the War and the 1940s, images needed to be produced which were specific to a particular publication. There was, in addition, the need for artwork generated by the illustrated magazines, and even by the *Daily Herald*. This suggested studio work, and rather than engage an agency Odhams established a studio of their own. We do not know exactly where it was, but it can be assumed that it was somewhere within the immediate proximity of Fleet Street and Long Acre. This would have given ready access to a pool of models. The output of the studio can be seen in books on cooking, knitting and dressmaking, and even in publications such as *Practical Plastics.* Very often the studio work concerned the making of a frontispiece illustration.

While it seems no longer possible to trace the exact location of the studio we do know that in the years immediately leading up to the war the studio manager was Edwin J.Embleton, who appears to have been personally responsible, both at this stage and later, for contracting nationally known artists to do work for Odhams. The artwork concerned came at first in the form of etchings and engravings on title pages and as chapter headings. Intricately designed and colourful endpapers also date from the early part of Embleton's time at the studio.

Shortly after the outbreak of hostilities, Embleton, together with senior Odhams colleagues such as Parack and Surrey Dane, was seconded to the newly created Ministry of Information. His role with the ministry was to direct the seventy strong General Production Department.He continued there until the end of the war, presumably using his artwork knowledge in the design and production for the ministry of posters and leaflets, many of which were actually printed at Odhams North Watford plant. Of all the current publishers Odhams seemed to have the most appropriate art and pictorial expertise to foster information – disinformation and other aspects of morale boosting.

With the end of the war Edwin Embleton returned to Odhams, this time occupying a post that was described as Art Editor. He had been awarded the MBE for his wartime services. By

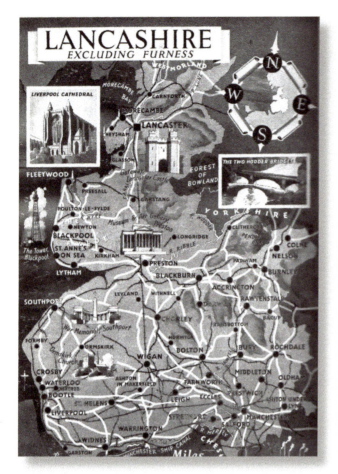

THE DREAM PIPER.
The piper of dreams draws all the children to his side and his music tells them of enchanted lands
where magic fills the air.

the late 1940s and early 1950s Odhams, as we shall see, were busily engaged in producing colour illustrated books on the British countryside. A sizeable proportion of the illustrations was made up of colour photographs, as there had been significant technological advances in both colour photography and colour printing processes. There was also, however, a considerable number of original watercolour paintings used.

It is hardly surprising that a number of the artists involved were those who had been producing artwork for the Ministry of Information, and whose work was therefore familiar to Embleton. Amongst the titles to which these artists contributed were numerous children's books such as **The Children's Wonder Book in Colour** and more significantly the nature books **The British**

Countryside in Colour, **The Nature Lover's Companion**, and **Nature Through the Seasons**. The latter was part of Odhams presentation at the South Bank Exhibition 1951-3. The watercolourists contributing included S.R.Badmin, John Nash, C.F.Tunnicliffe, and Raymond Sheppard, amongst many others whose etchings and paintings are still appreciated over half a century later.

The value placed by Odhams on colour artwork is best reflected by reproducing here the blurb on the pictorial dust-jacket of **Nature Through the Seasons**:

"The very essence of Nature's beauty and appeal lies in the glorious panorama of colour contrasts that delights the eye from season to season. It is fitting, therefore, that generous and effective

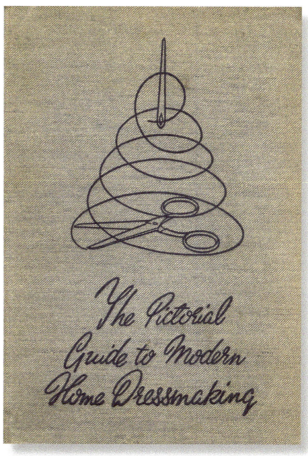

full-colour illustration of the highest standard should be the keynote of this new pictorial study of Nature at work through the year.

The frontispiece and no fewer than forty plates (including many attractive double-page spreads) present faithful reproductions, in four colour half-tone, of specially-commissioned paintings by thirteen leading contemporary artists. This superb series of colour plates – here published for the first time – includes the work of such notable artists as John Nash R. A., C.F. Tunnicliffe A. R. A., S. R. Badmin R. W. S., J. McIntosh Patrick, A. R. S. A., and Raymond Sheppard F. R. Z."

Informational art, fine illustration, contemporary photography and succinct symbols - all were represented by Odhams art departments.

The ideal suburban garden? Richard Sudell was an Odhams "garden expert'" over two decades

COMPLETE
FLOWER GARDENING
IN PICTURES

RICHARD SUDELL, F.I.L.A., F.R.H.S.

A comprehensive guide for the flower gardener.
Over 200 illustrations including 33 in colour.

GARDENING

In The 1930s the little piece of British countryside that increasing numbers of people were finding 'on their doorstep' (front and back) was their garden. Designing it, coping with it, digging, planting, caring for and improving it became matters of concern for growing numbers of the population who did not live in flats or urban terraces. New, suburban man (and woman), in mock-tudor semi or council house, had perforce to become a gardener. What in earlier years had been a fascinating hobby for the few had become, in fact had been becoming since the end of the previous century, an obligation for the new suburbans. This pattern of social change had begun near the start of Odhams' book publishing activities and went through various fluctuations in fashion and technique until the end of their existence as an independent unit in the 1970s. The firm had first become involved with the subject as early as 1923 when Geoffrey Henslow, organiser of the 1912 Chelsea Flower Show, was commissioned to author *Garden Construction*, a compendious volume which in its time became a basic guide. Odhams printed and published the book from their offices in Long Acre.

But the first serious venture in our period into what was then assumed, perhaps wrongly, to be a predominantly male activity was *Everybody's Gardening Guide* (1935?), part of a range of ' how-to' books which included the word 'Everybody's' in their title, perhaps as a sign that they were intended for consumption by the masses, across the classes and age-groups. However, they most probably ended up in the hands of the middle-class 'paterfamilias'.

This guide catered for the twin foci of the New Gardener — first, how to make the garden look good, its layout and design, and second, how to make part of it yield produce, basically fruit and vegetables. The advice was of a basic and practical kind and assumed presence in the garden to be at its maximum at weekends and on summer evenings.

Nor should we forget those without a garden who still wished to garden. For these there was the growing of plants indoors or in window boxes — and, of course, the allotment. For some decades before Odhams books appeared local councils, and some private landowners, had been letting out small plots of land to what was known at the time as the 'artisan class' living in gardenless tenements, flats or terraced houses. This system had flourished first in the industrial north, and soon spread to the whole country. Over the years the social makeup of allotment holders has changed, until, in our own time it is often the modestly affluent and ecologically aware who predominate in suburban allotments.

Odhams chose one man, Richard Sudell, to edit and produce its mainstream gardening books over a period of more than twenty years. Sudell maintained unchanging contents with similar chapter headings. His view of suburban gardens in the 1950s was essentially the same as in 1935. This may indeed have been a fair reflection of reality. With the exception of the worst years of the war, dealt with elsewhere, tastes and designs were much the same. It would be almost at the time of the demise of Odhams itself that traditional garden features, such as rockeries and herbaceous borders, began to lose their hold.

Many of Sudell's readers shared the public perception of gardening as a mystique subject, something for which select individuals had a knack or 'green fingers'. Perhaps as a result the second Odhams title on this subject was called *Secrets of Successful Gardening* (1939). The book was prepared, and possibly issued, during the opening stages of the war. In his introduction Sudell explains why he thinks gardening has become so important to so many people. He also attempts to de-mystify gardening and plant care by giving very simple rules for the vast majority of people who have 'modest' gardens of 'much less than an acre' of ground. (How times have changed!)

During the war years Sudell was again engaged to bring the subject of gardening up to date. The result was *Practical Gardening and Food Production in Pictures*. Although the gestation period may well have been the latter years of the war, and the wording of the title suggests that this was the case, the book may not have appeared until 1947. Rather oddly a 1950 edition still contains a chapter entitled 'How to adapt your garden in wartime'. Perhaps the atmosphere of the Cold War justified this.

Despite the wording of Sudell's foreword, the aim of the book remained essentially that of *Secrets of Successful Gardening*. In addition to the regular chapter headings this title contained sections on allotment gardening, on keeping rabbits and poultry, and on storing and preserving produce – all three areas suggesting a continuing wartime attitude to food production. The foreword is worth quoting in full, as much for language as for content:

This book is built on an entirely new principle. Every aspect of the art and science of gardening is presented through the medium of pictures and diagrams, so as to enable the veriest novice to undertake with confidence the cultivation of fruit, flowers and vegetables, and the care of poultry and rabbits. It has been said that one good picture is worth ten thousand words; this book is proof of the truth of that statement.

With it at his elbow, the gardener cannot go wrong, for he is not merely told, but also shown, what to do in every conceivable circumstance.

The emphasis now placed on diagrams and pictures mirrors the developing publishing and printing practices which are referred to elsewhere. In this book there is at least one diagram and one photograph on each page. Earlier publications had plentiful diagrams, but no photographs. The word 'practical' in the title also links gardening to the then current Odhams house-style, ranging from foundry practice to home decorating and knitting.

Many of the tenants in post-war housing built by local authorities, and a few of the private householders, inherited from the builders an empty garden plot or plots, front and back. If they were lucky the builders' rubbish had at least been hidden by a scattering of top-soil. There was also sometimes a token concrete path and post to facilitate the hanging out of washing. Converting this 'virgin' land to an attractive and productive garden was the main business of books such as the *Big Book of Gardening* (1956, and part of the 'Big Book' series). In its opening pages this publication tacitly assumed a clean slate. Adapting or altering an existing garden played a minor role, although some of the illustrations show 'cottages', rather than the by now ubiquitous 'semi', and these would presumably already have a garden of some kind if they were of any age. It was, design having been settled, the care and cultivation of plants that brought people to buy and use books of this kind. *The Big Book*, with its easy to read compartmentalized plant sections, bold alphabetical sub-headings, was essentially a book of reference, for long-term use. There is ample evidence too that such titles remained on family shelves and in general use well beyond the introduction of wipe-clean, laminated cards and ring folders in the 1970s and 1980s, and into the age of garden centres, the first of which may have opened as early as 1955, while the main blossoming was in the mid 1960s.

Though the gardens illustrated may now seem stiff and stereotyped with their trellises, sunken paved areas, rectilinear flower beds and inevitable rockery, the practical (to use the publisher's word) advice they give is still sound, and I find myself referring to them in my own gardening, stumbling as I do upon the forlorn pencil written notes made by earlier family generations. One major change has been that the liberal use of insecticides and poisons in the gardens seems to have lessened. We are also considering gardens where plastic and polythene are conspicuous by their absence. Another very obvious change, to judge by the illustrations, is that gardeners now dress for the task, and indeed garden centres, with their much wider choice of plants, encourage them to do so. The only concession our Odhams gardeners make is to wear gloves, and 'sturdy' shoes. In other respects they thought nothing it would seem, of undertaking double-digging wearing a collar and tie, waistcoat, jacket, and often a trilby. Illustrations from the period in other Odhams titles confirm that a brown coat was as far as some ideas of work clothes went, although there is also the suspicion that those people shown in the illustrations may have 'dressed up to have their photo taken'.

In the changing world of the mid-fifties Odhams produced a number of gardening-related titles as part of the Modern Living series. There were five titles altogether, two of which were in the mainstream gardening fold. The first was ***Pruning for Amateurs*** (1955). It was a recognition of a new generation of inexperienced householders who might have, or wish to have, fruit-trees in their (small) garden. To write the book Odhams engaged the help of a fruit expert well-known at the time, the aptly named Raymond Bush. Bush already had two successful 1940s Penguin handbooks on the subject, and one suspects that much of the information in this 1955 book is common to them. As with other books in this series the main aim was to demystify the subject, perceived, as we have said, by many as complex and 'technical'.

The second such title also involved a well-known character, the BBC's much loved voice of gardening – Fred Streeter. Again, the target was the so-called amateur gardener, and Streeter's prose was used to show exactly how easy and yet effective work in the garden could be, especially now that gardening help in the person of a gardener was difficult to obtain. The book was entitled ***Labour-saving Gardening*** (1956) a wording very much in tune with a mindset that was accepting newly appearing, and now cheaply available domestic appliances on the grounds that they were 'labour-saving'. Within a few years this attitude was to spread to garden appliances, but that was still to come.

The three other titles answered a need already discussed – gardening related activities without a garden. ***Gardening without a Garden*** (1955) dealt with the areas that were not strictly garden, nor yet indoors – window boxes, hanging baskets, and so forth. It also covered house plants, flower arrangements – and even artificial flowers. In many ways it reflected the social changes we have seen in the field of cookery. More people, both the elderly and the young single worker, were living alone, in accommodation where there was no garden. This book gave them ideas of the ways in which they could maintain at least some contact with the world of living plants. Plants they could tend themselves and take delight in.

In so far as it covered the areas it did it overlapped with a title which sold so well that it went into at least six reprints between 1958 and 1966. This was **The Care and Cultivation of Indoor Plants** (1958) by Violet Stevenson. Since most houses in the mid to late 1950s were not the double-glazed, centrally heated, air-conditioned places of today a great deal of her attention is given to keeping plants alive and well in what might be a hostile environment with draughts and wildly fluctuating temperatures. Some plants do better than others, obviously, at coping with this situation, and we have to remember that in 1958 the term 'house-plant' had only just become established. Stevenson writes:

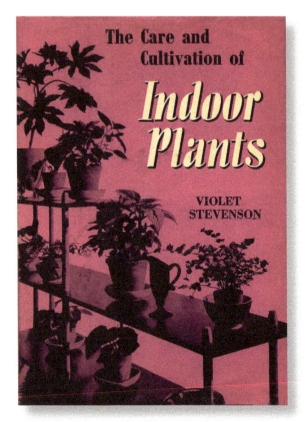

Odhams response to changing social patterns of accommodation and living.

What about those permanent plants, which, because of the publicity which has been given to them in all kinds of newspapers and magazines, have come to be known as the houseplants?

Towards these and other plants the book adopts a quaintly maiden aunt attitude, as though what were being cared for were pets or very small children. This indeed may have been the relationship some people had with their plants (cf.' Talk to your plants', 1980+). Nevertheless the book is a scientifically reliable guide, with a carefully composed care chart at the end.

The same author was engaged to produce at about the same time a book devoted to a more 'practical' application of garden produce – **Decorating with Plants and Flowers** (1963). It was a logical move sideways from the simple making of a garden to the addition of flair and fashion to the home. It was in some ways the bringing of the garden indoors, and it presaged the big boom in modern versions of the conservatory beloved of the Victorian well-to-do.

Two more echoes of a continuing interest in gardens appeared towards the end of the period covered by this survey. One came out in the late 'fifties, and the other in 1963-4. The Modern Living texts had been of a new (for Odhams), compact size. They were, curiously, rather like hardback paperbacks. Their size tended towards the pocket. They certainly looked more of the 1950's, as did Violet Stevenson's book.

The final flourish in the direction of gardening, however, used the much larger format of the 'Illustrated/In pictures' series. Datewise there is contact between the two, for Richard Sudell's **Complete Flower Gardening in Pictures** appeared in May, 1957. There were 190 pages with the text broken up by an enormous number of illustrations, hand-drawn mono, colour plates and mono photographs. It touched upon all the most popular garden flowers of the period, and naturally also included garden planning, preparation and arrangement. It was a typical product of the time – part coffee-table and part reference. The colour plates alone are most impressive, and represent Odhams at their best. The printers used were Morrison and Gibb. It was not, however, simply all about the cultivation of garden flowers, as the final paragraph of Sudell's introduction makes clear:

Flowers, both in the garden and in the home, have so many uses. They cheer the sick and encourage the healthy by their colour and fragrance. Like music, flowers speak a common language throughout all nations. It is significant that when national leaders meet, they frequently garland each other with flowers. To have flowers in profusion in one's garden to cut and give to friends on special occasions, is surely one of our greatest pleasures. We hope these pages will help you to grow, enjoy and share flowers to the full.

Times change, and it is noticeable that what the author considers an average size garden now seems very large indeed.

Violet Stevenson's ***Decorating with Plants and Flowers*** (1963) is what might be called a practical application of her previous book for Odhams. It is a general text on flower-arranging, with 20-odd excellent colour plates. Such a well-produced book, again in the large format, must, however, have had many serious rivals in the new leisure-centred world of the affluent 1960s.

The final gardening book is in fact a general survey of garden types throughout history, literally from the Garden of Eden to the almost present-day. ***Gardens through the Ages*** (1964) is an Odhams English language version of an original Dutch/ Flemish text, and was printed in Belgium, one of the few Odhams books to be printed outside the UK. ***Time and Tide*** reviewed it as a children's book, and it is indeed in the largest format normally reserved for art books and children's picture books. Yet, curiously, the target audience is hard to identify from the text which is at times academic, but also at others more obviously addressed to children, albeit bookish and intellectual children or adolescents. The book is lavishly illustrated, all the illustrations hand-drawn and, in retrospect, all 1950's and 1960's in style. ***Time's*** reviewer admitted that adults would also find it interesting when prevented from gardening by a rainy afternoon! There is a modicum of low-level identification and cultivation advice that keeps this title in the gardening fold.

If we think of the publication date of the Big Book of Gardening (1956) we can see that almost to the end Odhams maintained a balance between mainstream gardening information and advice and the more peripheral aspects, represented by the three last published titles. This two-pronged policy reflects what we shall see with needlecraft and associated activities.

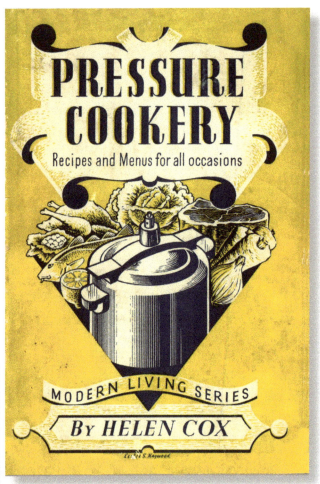

Odhams were in the forefront of reflecting technological change in the kitchen.

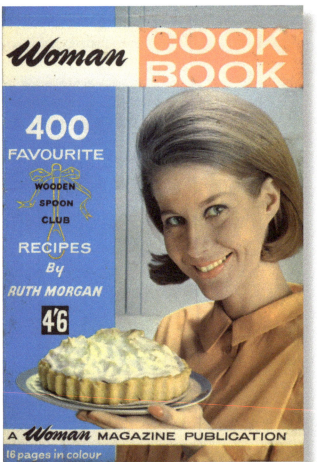

The magazine derivatives played their part in spreading cooking ideas to as many readers as possible.

COOKERY

In the period between 1935 and 1970 Odhams produced a dozen or so reference books devoted to cooking, as we can see from the following representative list:

1936 Cookery and Home Management
1937 The Cookery Book
1938 Modern Cookery Illustrated
1947 Home Cookery Illustrated
1954 Commonsense Cooking and Eating
1955 Pressure Cookery
1956 Philip Harben's Cookery Encyclopaedia
1967 Practical Cookery for All

There were, as we can see, a number of different angles from which the subject was approached. Very often the nature and contents of the book were the result of the influence of external factors. In a number of cases Odhams seem to have been either directly or indirectly commissioned as publishers by industries or manufacturers. *The Electric Cookbook* (1931-38) went through a number of impressions and represented a reaction to change and development in kitchen technology. This was similarly true of *Pressure Cookery* of 1955. By the time *Philip Harben's Cooking Encyclopaedia* and *The Woman Cookbook* appeared the refrigerator, for example, was an established feature of at least middle-class homes, albeit lower down the income scale the cold larder or pantry and the bottling jar still dominated the storage of food.

There was a break in the regular output of cookery books between 1938 and 1947, and a slightly shorter pause between the latter year and 1954. There was a natural underlying reason for the first break, and that was the reaction to the shortages and deprivation caused by the war. The second may have been the result of coping with the restrictions of rationing, both of food and of the paper needed to produce the books themselves.

Eating habits and what might be called 'dietary politics' changed, as might be expected, quite dramatically over the almost thirty years 1936 -64. A perusal of the recipes, however, reveals a continuity of favourites, both in main courses and desserts. It is also noticeable how the war, the presence in Britain of many thousands of US service personnel, together later with large numbers of German and Italian POWs, and, towards the end of the conflict the movement of British service personnel around the world, a kind of enforced 'foreign travel', introduced the British to new and hitherto exotic dishes. We should note here the increasing use of the adjective 'continental' to suggest exciting or out of the ordinary as far as food dishes were concerned. This often also reflected the growing habit of eating out in restaurants with a 'foreign' cuisine. Previously the domain of the upper and upper middle classes this was now slowly spreading down the social scale.

The focus had changed from what was needed to feed the family to how to produce new and attractive dishes. Cookery was ceasing to be just something every good wife should be able to do to something that all the family could take part in, even the husband and father. Philip Harben's TV cookery programme played a significant part in this. Early post-war TV was watched on a large scale to begin with as a novelty and as a whole family activity, and in this respect there can be no doubt that activities divided by traditional gender attitudes were now viewed across the divide. Men were willy-nilly involved in cookery by simply watching it and thereby seeing what they had previously only enjoyed on the plate.

Odhams' output reflected these changes - though the appearance as late as 1967 of the title **Practical Cookery for All** did contain echoes of the 1930s.

In general there were two strands evident in Odhams' approach to cookery. Nowhere is this more obvious than if we compare **Cookery Illustrated and Household Management** (1936) and Ruth Morgan's **Woman Cookbook** (1964). They are very different books both to handle and to look at. The first is a (somewhat old-fashioned) hardback compendium of some 750 pages, of which 450 odd are concerned with everyday recipes, and the remainder, as the title suggests, with household management, which ranged in subject matter from preserving to dieting and first aid. The editor, Elizabeth Craig, was a known cookery 'name', and her foreword accurately describes the balance of recipes:

Many cookery books fail in taking for granted that the house wife knows more than she does about cookery. Special care has been taken in this book to describe the recipes as clearly as possible. It has been written to appeal equally to the experienced and inexperienced housewife, and even a novice in cookery should be able to follow the recipes without any difficulty.

All directions are given in the order in which they are to be carried out, and the time required for cooking each dish is clearly indicated. The number of persons for whom the dish is designed is shown at the beginning of the recipes, and the quantities can be increased or decreased proportionately for larger or smaller families.

Remember that although a list of household utensils has been given with each recipe in order to simplify the preparation of food, the dishes can sometimes be prepared without many of them. On the other hand, cooking in a kitchen with up-to-date equipment usually takes less time than when makeshifts are used. I am glad to be able to present to housewives not only a large number of modern recipes, but also a large number of old favourites, which I have often been asked for and which I have found very few books carry. There is one thing husbands won't be able to say any more if their wives use this cookery book, and that is that they can't get the dishes mother used to make.

A look at the opening list of contents suggests the tenor of the book, and the closing chapters reinforce this.

A Guide to this book
>The Technique of Cooking
>Keeping Down the Household Bills
>Making the most of leftovers
>Dodges to prevent waste
>Cooking in Emergencies

* * * * * *

Household Management
>Entertaining without a Maid
>To Save Labour in the Home
>The Kitchen and its Equipment
>Table Ware
>Household Linen
>Marketing
>The Storeroom, the Larder
>Washing Up

Household Hints
by Florence Caulfield Hewlett
>Hints on First-Aid, Health and Beauty

So we can see that this particular compendium like book was as much about running a home as about recipes, though the latter were still given a goodly proportion of the space available.

As a matter of interest, **Modern Cookery Illustrated**, which came out two years later, had a very similar format, but had dropped the rather Victorian, Mrs Beeton-ish, final 250-300 pages on household management. Perhaps that is why it was deemed 'modern', for the recipes seem reasonably familiar, but gone were the considerations listed above about managing without domestics in the new circumstances. Both these books 'ancient' and 'modern' were substantial reference volumes, bound in board and grey flecked cloth, weighty, intended, presumably to be read from the kitchen table or work surface rather than consulted when held in the hand, as we can see from the frontispiece photograph in **Modern Cookery**. However well the cooking went both these volumes would be too cumbersome to hold and read.

By contrast the **Woman Cookbook** (1964) was a completely different animal. In the first place the format was different – it looked and felt like a paperback, though slightly larger than a regular Penguin. It had a brightly coloured wipe-dry cover, and could be held easily with one hand while the other did the stirring, mixing, seasoning or whatever, or even operated the switch on whatever new kitchen appliance was being used. It was truly portable in the sense in which the others had not been. It also represented a new kind of book – one which was a spin-off from another publication, in this case an illustrated magazine. The magazine in question was, of course, **Woman**, one of the most successful in the Odhams' portfolio. The introduction, by Ruth Morgan, the **Woman** cookery editor, is revealing about the make-up of the book:

In this book you will find the recipes that are loved best and made most by members of **Woman** *Wooden Spoon Club This club is unique. The only qualification is to be a reader of* **Woman** *magazine. There are eight million members. And through the pages of* **Woman** *the club provides an unequalled centre for the exchange of cookery ideas and know-how. The Wooden Spoon Club is equipped with a superb kitchen, and staffed by a team of highly qualified experts. It is here that the weekly cookery features in* **Woman** *are thought out and created. To this club comes an enormous correspondence, from readers: recipes, ideas and opinions. From the food industry: a constant flow of information about new products, and exciting ways to cook with existing ones. All this information is sifted, tabulated and checked. The result is a very special cookery service to the readers of* **Woman**. *Now we're happy to invite everyone to share our favourite recipes. We have great confidence in them because they are Wooden Spoon Club tested. They are planned to help everybody who cooks, from the busy mother of a family to the girl with a home and a job. And they are arranged so that you can easily find the answer to your own particular catering problem. We hope this book will bring variety and new pleasures to your table.*

It was declaredly aimed at a cross-section of (women) cooks, ranging from grandmothers to grand-daughters – including dishes traditional and modern, and even including a chapter entitled 'Going continental'. It was expected that the readership would consist, as we can see, of the eight million odd members of the magazine's own cookery club – The Wooden Spoon Club (ingenious or deliberately ambiguous?). Such loyalty readership activities in the 1960s harks back uncannily to the **Daily Herald's** loyalty subscriber campaigns of thirty years earlier with book coupons as stimulants. The wording of the introduction also demonstrates just what kind of special relationship the editor/publisher was attempting to build up with the readership. As a 4/6d paperback this volume was intended to widen the audience, and would probably increase the circulation of **Woman** into the bargain.

We shall notice how, over the period we are

Over the years the change
in the nation's nutrition;
from the sparse, appliance
-free 1950's kitchen to the
exotic menu of the 1960s,
are clearly illustrated
through Odhams
housekeeping and cookery
publications

COOKING BY PICTORIAL LESSONS

surveying, Odhams were striving gradually to give what might be called its 'household books' a modern image. With growing prosperity in the mid 1950s, smaller format, more accessible books were needed, cheap, portable and easy to follow.

With this in mind a series was started in 1953 entitled **Modern Living**. A rapid perusal of the titles – **How to Choose and Enjoy Wine**, **Country Wines**, **Commonsense Cooking and Eating**, **Pressure Cookery**, and significantly **The Art of Conversation**, followed rather oddly by **The Child's First Five Years** – throws light on several factors – first the series was not just about cookery, but very much about lifestyle, about entertaining, bringing up a family. It was a new middle-income, car-owning target readership, although council house tenants who thought of themselves as upwardly mobile would also be amongst those who parted with their 8/6d for these slim volumes. This series went on in reprints until 1958 and represented in a way instruction manuals on 'how to have it so good'.

A further light on social change is provided by the way **Commonsense Cooking and Eating**, for example, recognised that since the war, in the cities and towns at least, more people were living alone. The first forty pages of the book are taken up by the following chapters:

Young Person Living Alone;
One Room Cookery;
Menus for the Single Room Cook,
and towards the end of the book are chapters entitled,
Elderly Persons and Menus for Elderly Persons.

Flats were now more available in urban areas, often in blocks as part of re-housing or urban clearance. With the expansion of tertiary education there were more students, and they were increasingly living in bedsits with minimal cooking facilities, as university hostels could not keep pace with demand.

So it is easy to see that Odhams' approach to such a basic subject as cookery was two-stream. The first of the twin prongs was to keep on producing 'standard' encyclopaedic cookery reference books, culminating in **Practical Cookery for All** (1967). These standard works updated their recipes round the fringe, and always took time out to cover new advances in kitchen equipment. The second prong was to react to social change in terms of a life-style re-jig to a situation without 'domestics'. And also to react to changes in attitude to 'foreign food', and to produce books which reflected these changes and integrated them into the world of cookery. The younger housewife or the bachelor cook was the target of the second prong, yet we must bear in mind that as far as social attitudes were concerned these books all still see cookery as a predominantly female preserve.

The male in the kitchen is reflected in **Philip Harben's Cookery Encyclopaedia** (1955) which we have referred to in passing above. The book was an obvious TV spin-off. As we can see, the introduction underlined that this was a standard cookery book, but built around a popular and much-loved TV personality, whose weekly programme (to begin with in black and white for most viewers) had a considerable following. Though before the war there had been very few people with access to a television, by the turn of the 'fifties into the 'sixties it was estimated that three quarters of households had a TV set.

Harben was the first in a line that was to go on to include, Fanny and Johnny Cradock, Delia Smith, and a line that is still continuing to produce cooking celebrities in the 21st century. Harben had begun with a weekly TV programme as early as 1946, when Britain was still deep in austerity and tight food rationing. Though the series itself ended in 1951 he continued to appear in one-off programmes until the mid 1960s. Other publishers were producing books of his hints and recipes, and given his high profile Odhams were lucky to acquire this title, and efforts were made to ensure that the cook was visible in a large proportion of the black and white photographs. In other respects, though, the book was orthodox – truly encyclopaedic and alphabetically laid out. It dealt on the one hand with basic information, such as an explanation of the meaning of the word 'frying' and at the other end of the scale, an esoteric vegetable such as salsify. The book also contained food and drink maps, and an English-French-English culinary vocabulary. This was the age when 'foreign dishes' still meant in the main continental European cuisine, basically French and Italian.

Despite the almost patronising nature of some of the very basic information covered the tone is unmitigatedly middle-class and even 1930-ish. How many people reading in the late 'fifties would have any idea of what a thesaurus was, and how many would have to use a dictionary to get to the meaning of 'recondite'? Also the juxtaposition of the words 'modern', 'practical' and 'home' is almost consciously humorous in view of Odhams long term titling policy. In the lengthy foreword Harben talks of his experience in writing the book, and explains that it is intended to be encyclopaedic, and a reference source. Then he continues:

The first question I had to decide when planning this work was: how much should be included? For the subject is so vast. I decided to include as far as possible everything that a modern practical home cook might reasonably want to know, but nothing that appeared to me to be too recondite. The next question was: at what length should each subject be treated, how exhaustively? Here again I decided that the most logical thing was to give each subject the length that it appeared to need, no more and no less, having regard to its importance in the scale of things. If you are looking for novelties, or for original Harben recipes, you will not find them in this book. It is not that kind of book. It is intended to be a text book, a reference book, a thesaurus of established culinary knowledge. Being in alphabetical order, the book needs no index at the end – it is self-indexing. So, to find the answer to any question, just look up the operative word, and I hope that you will find the answer. Anyway, here's wishing you the best of luck!

It is interesting to learn that Harben started writing the book two years before publication, when the social standards of the pre-war middle class were still in the ascendant. The contrast with the almost matey stance taken up by the **Woman Cookbook** ten years later is vivid. The book is also significant in that it brings together two streams of Odhams publishing philosophy: reference works and contemporary fashion.

Those books in the **Modern Living** series mentioned above which reflected the broad area of food and eating and drinking – **Country Fare**; **Country Wines**, and **How to Choose and Enjoy Wine** – all had a potential readership which was largely of the middle class, whose tastes were becoming more expansive under the influence of media exposure of wider cuisine (as represented by programmes like Philip Harben's ?) The two books on wine both first appeared in 1953 and went on being reprinted until 1958. Country Fare first appeared in 1956, and it is a link between the subject of cookery its widest sense and the countryside of Britain, in all its aspects.

Mary Aylett, the author of **Country Fare**, makes it obvious from the beginning of the book that she is aware of writing to a Britain which is markedly different from that of the years of austerity, and is becoming more so. The opening chapter – 'Domestic Revolution' sets an objective in its first few lines:

Political revolutions are made amidst clamour.
The domestic revolution altered the physique, the
customs and the minds of men all over the Western
world, and it has been largely ignored…

In fact nearly all the opening pages of the book are concerned with social change – and only indirectly with food and drink. More than anything else in this section Aylett concentrates on the change of life-style for the rural population. Radio, television, private transport, all played significant roles in raising desire horizons. Increased affluence now made some of the goals achievable – and this was reflected in diet, choice of food items, entertaining and eating out.

Life had changed also for those most concerned with food and cooking – women:

The girls who had once, as a matter of course
gone into service, not only from necessity, but
as training for their own married lives became
typists or factory hands, working fixed hours, and
often keeping to their jobs after marriage…

In the country farmhouse (and the manor house where it still existed) –

Today things are very different. Domestic
help is often one inexperienced maid or
even only a daily charwoman…

Aylett focuses on the ready availability of country fruits and herbs – the cheapness and simplicity of 'living from the hedgerows'.The solid, staple, traditional meat-centred dishes of the 1930s cookbooks suddenly seem a very, very long way away. Canning and pre-wrapping are already present as Aylett writes, and supermarket ready meals are only just over the horizon. War shortages

and post-war austerity had in a curious way made some pre-war dishes seem old-fashioned, and in an increasingly affluent, fashion- and media-led society, sober dinner parties had perhaps less of a role to play. Eating out became important, partly because food tastes had developed away from the everyday. For many the weekly joint and Friday fish and chips were still the culinary high spots of the week, but, as Aylett points out, expressing an acute foresight of what the pressures of supermarket shopping would produce:

The poor are more subject to the pressure of
circumstance than the rich, and the unedu-
cated more at the mercy of propaganda…

Nevertheless, **Country Fare** acts as a link (presaging as it does 'the Good Life') with two other important streams of Odhams titles, which are dealt with in separate chapters: The Countryside of Britain, and Gardening.

A 'crest' devised from kitchen equipment and foodstuffs for Modern Cookery Illustrated features old-fashioned meat grinders.

Rooms which are on the sunny side of the house should be furnished in "cool" colours, such as blues and greens. But a scheme of this kind without any of the gayer, "warmer" shades would be very un-interesting, so a touch of a complete contrast is in-troduced to give a hint of gaiety, as in the blue scheme with the red cushion on the right. Yellow is a colour which will give a feeling of sunlight to rooms that have no natural sun. This is illustrated below in the yellow and green scheme, with the contrast-ing mauve curtains to enrich the scheme.

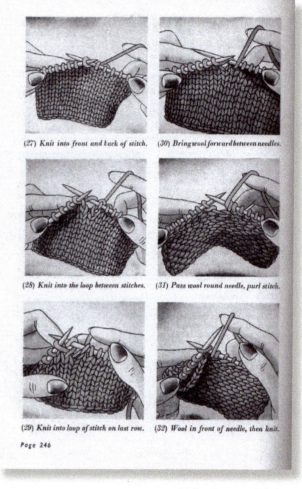

(27) *Knit into front and back of stitch.*

(30) *Bring wool forward between needles.*

(28) *Knit into the loop between stitches.*

(31) *Pass wool round needle, purl stitch.*

(29) *Knit into loop of stitch on last row.*

(32) *Wool in front of needle, then knit.*

Page 246

Whether explaining interior design theory or needlecraft skills and techniques, comprehensive and helpful illustrations invariably accompanied the instructive text.

NEEDLECRAFT, KNITTING AND DRESSMAKING

As far as this subject is concerned two things need to be said at the outset: first, nowhere are fluctuations in taste and fashion more likely to be revealed than in this area, and second, since the demise of Odhams in the 1970s there have been available ever increasing amounts of imported cheap ready-made clothes, and an increased application of man-made fibres. These two latter factors have meant that less and less people are making their own and their family's clothes.

There is, for example, a whole world of fashion change between *The Big Book of Needlecraft* (1938) and *Fashion and Dressmaking* (1962). This is evident not only in the clothing styles and the make-up of the models, made especially vivid by the contrast between the line drawings of the first book, and the frontispiece photograph of the second, but also in the total size, shape and purpose of the two, and this despite, or perhaps because symptomatically, the fact that the second title is limited to the application of needlecraft.

The Big Book, in common with other titles in the *Big* series, is intended to be comprehensive in coverage, making it necessary to have only one book dealing with a range of related subjects, from embroidery to upholstery, and from knitting to leather-work and glove making. The book has 570 pages of text, and an index. The contents cover some 30-odd subdivisions of the general subject of needlecraft. There is little scope for choice of interesting patterns, as each section is necessarily fairly short and concentrates on a simple explanation of method and equipment. It is not intended, as many later titles are, to deal with questions of design. Even so skirt lengths and shoulder lines are very obviously different from those in post-war titles that came after the 'paper starvation' of 1941 onwards. *The Big Book* did have in common with some subsequent titles the fact that it was produced bound in cloth-covered boards. In the course of the '40s and '50s cookery and needlecraft titles tended to receive this treatment.

Two years and one month elapsed before the appearance of *The Pictorial Guide to Modern Home Dressmaking* (1940). This passage of time was sufficient to push hems up and shoulders out, and to push the country from phoney war to the brink of total war, upon which followed austerity in clothing, and a restricted supply of paper and skilled workers for printing. Squeezed in before this gloom descended *The Pictorial Guide* is just that, rich in photographs, some amusingly showing women modelling dresses echoing a time that was rapidly drifting into the pre-war past. It now seemed quaint to see some of them holding cigarettes in cigarette-holders. It has 300-odd pages, a glossary and an index. It includes sections on tailoring, lingerie, sportswear and 'utility clothes'. This latter section, as though presaging the androgenous and anonymous siren suits to come, includes what is described as a one-piece 'unity suit' (shades of *1984*). Significantly, there is also a section on renovating clothes and re-using old materials – true re-cycling.

Miraculously, considering the situation regarding the availability of paper, two books on knitting appeared during the war years. *Knitting for All Illustrated* came out at one of the darkest periods, in October, 1941. All the factors that had affected **Home Dressmaking** a year earlier were now in full play, exacerbated by fuel shortages for heating. The 320 pages of **Knitting for All** therefore contain no surprises. There is much emphasis on 'warm' and 'cosy', as well as the conventional 'smart'. With one or two exceptions there is a dearth of bright colours, and 'serviceable' and 'useful' are frequently encountered epithets. This was, and would continue to be for a decade or so, a society where the purchase of new clothes for any member of the family would be a rare occurrence. Hence there is a 35 page section on remaking and 'making do'. Some three years later a further similar title appeared **Knitted Garments for All** (1944). Despite the fact that the outcome of the war, at least in Europe, was at this stage no longer in doubt, this publication reinforced all that had been in its predecessor, and added new patterns and new ideas. It seemed that austerity still held sway, and keeping warm was at least as important as being 'smart'.

There followed a four year gap, during which time clothing was still rationed, along with many other items, including haberdashery, and patterns and materials had to be acquired as and when. In 1947 Odhams returned to this subject with **Practical Family Knitting Illustrated**, this was in fact a reprint of a title which had appeared several years earlier. The title-page and style of the book had been brought into line with the late 'forties. The authorial partnership of Margaret Murray and Jane Koster had also been involved in other Odhams knitting books, and it was a pairing which obviously worked well. This title claimed to be 'a comprehensive book of knitted garments for everyone'. The **Illustrated** of the actual title is entirely of the period, and virtually every garment is modelled in photographs, some in colour. The print fonts used reflect the types used in Odhams' illustrated womens magazines of the period, and

unlike sister publications it was produced in plain boards.

In media terms the late 1940s was predominantly a period of the wireless and the cinema. In fact listening to the radio in front of a coal fire was very conducive to knitting. Everything involved could be contained in the lap, and there can be no doubt about its popularity at the time amongst women of all ages. It was, after all, one way of providing clothes reasonably cheaply when times were hard. Patterns or ideas for patterns often came from what was new out of Hollywood as much as from magazine sources. Knitting, as we know, was however only one part of the overall picture, and in 1948 a 'companion' volume appeared for sewing and needlecraft. This was **Practical Home Needlecraft in Pictures**. The titling reflects the atmosphere of economy on the home front current at the time. It is in the main an instructional book, concerned with stitchery, and aimed at embroiderers and quilters, rather than dressmakers and seamstresses. To that extent the interpretation of needlecraft in the **Big Book of Needlecraft** had been drastically narrowed down. Within just a few years areas covered by this 300 plus page title, such as embroidery, patchwork and quilting were to become the field of an ever decreasing number of committed enthusiasts – a specialist field concerned with what was coming to be regarded as 'country crafts'. Yet our 1948 book makes assumptions that will soon prove to be outdated – such as:

'In some form or another it (needlecraft) is used daily in every household, and the elementary principles are taught in most girls' schools.'

Thus runs the introductory page. Further on we read:

'Most women have, at some time in their lives, embroidered something, even if it is only the brush

and comb bag initial of their school days'.

In the decade that followed the picture given by these remarks began rapidly to fade, though there is enough austerity left for the opening remarks on patchwork to have a convincing ring of truth:

> *'The needlewoman of today prides herself in turning every tiny piece of material to good account. Bedspreads, cushion-covers, tea-cosies, aprons, jackets, housecoats, needlework bags, these are but a few of the things that can be made economically with scraps of material pieced together in a decorative way.'*

Thus the book can be seen as a valuable aid to helping households to cope with the (relative) hardships of those years. But in a great many other respects it can hardly be seen as forward-looking.

Odhams, again using Murray and Koster, brought out in the same year a title much more forward-looking, pattern-centred, and less instructive of the basic principles. This book was called simply ***Knitting Illustrated***. At 250 pages it was shorter than many of its sisters, though it contained suggestions for more than 90 garments or sets of items such as place-mats. The photographic illustrations were acceptable, but the coloured and black and white drawings were already redolent of the early 1950s, and were thus presumably a selling line. The book already had a sense of gaiety and movement which made its immediate predecessors seem rather stuffy. Something of its time is still there, however, in the presentation of patterns for knitted underwear and swimming costumes (remember how embarrassing when coming out of the water?), and curios such as how to knit yourself – or someone else? – a 'snug, smart skullcap'. One non-Odhams publication of the period even included an illustration of a knitted flying suit! Patterns for bed-socks speak volumes about cold linoleum floors and draughty bedrooms – the very smell of such rooms comes

out of the pages of the book, just as it does out of those published in the war years.

Two years later a further title on knitting appeared, also less introductory and more applied, of no more than 250 pages, and with only one colour illustration. It was ***Knitted Garments for the Family*** (1950) and was prepared by Dorothy Beckett, a regular Odhams author. It contained over 80 patterns, and although some of these reflected a rapidly passing world with their knitted underwear, camiknickers, 'pantees' (sic), and references to older women as 'matrons', the book nevertheless began to show the New Look impinging on shoulders, skirt lengths and so forth. The childrens' patterns, particularly for the very young, went on being acceptable for another decade before the introduction of cheaper, imported, mass-produced clothes for the very young in the 'sixties.

Making clothing at home was, however, still much in the mind of the average housewife, and dressmaking in particular was beginning to become a matter of keeping pace with rapidly changing fashions. There had obviously been quite a number of fashion changes in dressmaking since the beginning of the 1940s. Now, in 1952, Odhams brought out ***Complete Dressmaking in Pictures***. The titling was interesting – it suggested a comprehensive survey of techniques and the use of machinery much in line with ***The Complete Home Handyman***, and similar books discussed elsewhere. It was attempting to answer all needs. 'In pictures', echoing the countryside books of the same decade, meant in fact illustrated with plenty of sketches and mono and coloured photographs. The patterns and designs were now more relaxed and had absorbed a New Look sense of style. The book was reprinted in 1955 with slight alterations. Both printings were redolent of the optimism of the 'New Elizabethan Age'.

Two years later, and after a lapse of some 19 years, Odhams produced a successor to the **Big Book of Needlecraft**. Comparisons between the earlier book and the new **Encyclopaedia of Needlecraft Illustrated** (1957) are revealing. Like its predecessor the Encyclopaedia covers a wide range of aspects of needlecraft, but its main emphasis is on techniques of plain sewing and on dressmaking. Other expected areas like knitting, soft furnishing (a new term?), mending and soft toy making, are also included, but out have gone 'New Collars for Old Dresses', household renovations, upholstery, glove making, leathercraft and "Useful Washing Hints". In general there is much less of an atmosphere of make do and mend, and more and more emphasis on fashion and style. The country was, after all, still going through the period of euphoria surrounding the 1951 Festival of Britain six years previously. Design was in the air, particularly in home décor, with crockery, wall papers and fabrics taking the lead. There are other respects in which this book, as might be expected, is a different animal. It is very brightly coloured and attractively bound. The format is slightly larger than the **Big Book**, the very outward appearance of which now seemed dated and pre-war. The quality of the paper and print is also superior, and marks the progress of Odhams in producing books which are, some fifty or more years later, undoubtedly still used as reference sources by those involved in crocheting, embroidery and quilting as craft activities.

In the vocabulary of its descriptions the book turns again and again to the word 'gay' in its original, single, meaning of happy, carefree, brightly coloured and, often, young. This word alone seems to encapsulate the 'fifties. Ups and downs and changes in fashion, and economic circumstances were to follow, but the **Encyclopaedia** is a product of this innocent pre-stage.

Five years later there appeared what might be seen as a culminating title in this dressmaking series – **Odhams Fashion and Dressmaking** (1962). As the title suggests this was more than a book about the techniques of dressmaking and the choice of patterns. Instead it was answering not just these needs, but also public curiosity about just what constituted 'fashion' and how it came about. As a subsidiary question there was also the exact meaning of the term 'design'. The book in fact stood at the very threshold of the concept of 'designer clothes'.

The foreword to this title pitches the book at 'those who have a feeling for fashion and flair'. The writer continues with some possibly unfair comments, and she presumably includes earlier Odhams books in her remarks:

> *…I can only say that I wish this book had been around when I was trying painfully to learn from books or pamphlets written in incomprehensible jargon with strangely ugly and still more puzzling diagrams…*

The writer was Professor of Fashion Design at the Royal College of Art – a new chair, and an indication of the esteem now given to the subject. Before the book moved on to the process of design and dressmaking techniques there followed six pages of consideration of the question – What is fashion? There was an assessment of public reaction to fashion and of the role of the media, the press, daily and Sunday, and fashion dedicated glossy magazines such as **Vogue**, **Harpers** and **Vanity Fair**. Attention was also drawn to the role of the 'new players' – fashion gurus such as Dior, Givenchy, Balenciaga, Chanel and Worth. There was a sense of urgency and rapid change in this introductory section with its references to sputniks and automation. Earlier Odhams books – be they on knitting, dressmaking or needlecraft, were often truly instructional, but they were seldom what this early 'sixties title was trying to be – inspirational. In this respect it is fascinating to note from the dust-jacket of this 1962 title that the **Big Book of Needlecraft** was still being marketed! In addition to 'doing it the correct way' the writers of **Fashion and Dressmaking**, Renee and Julian Robinson, wanted the dressmaking housewife or student to know where their cotton or silk fabric came from, and to know the composition and uses of synthetic fibres. It was an area of importance barely touched on by earlier titles restricted as their readers were to indifferent supplies of wool and cotton. There is in this last book a real sense of the world beginning to open out.

Warm without being bulky, this bedjacket is worked in crazy-pattern crochet. The straight "cut" and magyar-style sleeves give ease of fit, the only fastenings being the ribbon ties at neck, waist and sleeves. The instructions are on page 431.

From practical apparel to home decor, Odhams covered both for many years.

Can the humour of
this studio shot have
escaped anyone?
It certainly has
not escaped the
models used!

Something to occupy every member of the family. The section on flowercraft commences on page 39, leatherwork on page 57 and basketwork on page 113.

PRACTICAL MAN
(AND PRACTICAL WOMAN)

Practical Man, and later Practical Woman, were the invention of Odhams Press. He, and she, were modestly affluent and lived in or near Metroland, or in one of the suburban sprawls that now surrounded most British cities. They might even be tenants in one of the new council houses, or possibly reasonably well educated industrial or agricultural workers.

Two social currents had come together to bring these people into existence, and to make them a target market for Odhams. One was the already mentioned emphasis on the development of self-reliance, an emphasis placed in the 1930s by the boy scouts and other youth movements, religious and political. The other was the growing awareness of style and fashion design for living, a current now flowing through much wider sections of society. Yet, more importantly for our purposes and those of Odhams, not everyone could afford the cost of having work done for them. Economic circumstances in the 1930s were still constrained, household budgets, even in Metroland, were tight. One obvious answer to the demands of these converging currents was to be 'practical' (or, as we now put it – DIY).

The desire for this kind of practical ability also promoted two other terms in titling – 'handy' and 'home'. The popular expression 'He (or she) is handy about the home' has possibly now been replaced by 'My partner is good at DIY'. Twenty-five or so volumes related to this kind of titling appeared from Odhams over the period 1938-60. They all contained the word 'practical' in their titles, and the subjects chosen for the exercise

of this practicality ranged from gardening to book-keeping. Even volumes which did not contain the word 'practical' in their title touched on this subject.

As one might expect there was a strong gender divide between perceived male activities such as decorating, woodwork and automobile engineering, and those perceived as areas where the woman could be practical, knitting and cookery, for example. It is easy to make fun of this in retrospect, but it reflected the then current social attitudes and also contemporary educational practice.

The word 'handy' occurred in seven of the titles from this range. It was a sign of the times that the middle-class and lower middle-class family was expected, for economic reasons, to be its own lawyer and counsellor, and to turn its hand to repairing its own car, radio and television, even to have a go at quite complex plumbing and electrical matters, all situations where in the present day we call in an 'expert'! In a way, Odhams 'practical' books acted as the internet of their day, offering advice and instruction on a wide range of subjects at the flick of a page.

It is reasonably obvious that a great deal of the titling has to do with marketing postures, and in this respect it is interesting to note that the word 'home' occurs in at least 15 of the books from this selection, e.g. *The Practical Home Doctor*. This latter reflecting at least two background factors – first a topical note at the time, the 1940s, when the provision of health services was a national issue, and secondly that the book formed a repository of advice, help and information instantly accessible within the home. There would be no need in an emergency to be, as the jargon of the time put it, 'stumped'. The ideal of the 'home' titles was that they should form a bank of information on a wide variety of subjects, readily accessible without recourse to an 'expert', or a free library, or a course in adult education. It reflected back in fact to the original intention of promoting self-sufficiency and practical know-how.

As time went by and post-war Britain drifted towards the New Look and the Festival of Britain (1951) many subtle changes in social behaviour were taking place, too numerous to be listed here. An awareness of some of these changes was expressed in Odhams' titling policy. It was realised that a number of the reference books that had appeared in the period 1930-1945 had been overtaken by events, and in the post-war world appeared fusty and outdated. Subtle changes in social behaviour are very well illustrated by two books with almost identical titles which appeared ten years apart in 1938 and 1948. The books concerned were *The Practical Handyman* and *The Practical Home Handyman*. The decade had been an eventful one with war, shortages and rationing preserving some make do and mend habits in aspic and yet other events creating behavioural changes and expectations. The tools involved in both titles were the same, with no evidence of power tools. Whereas the 1938 book envisaged readers building their own work-shed the post war publication assumed it to be already there. The earlier book also went to some lengths to explain the different kinds of wood, but this section had been omitted in 1948, when presumably no great variety of timber was yet available.

The later book was more concerned with renovation and 'modernizing', specifically the front porch and the bathroom. In the garden maintenance section continuity reigned, and every modest rectangular plot needed its trellis, though the veranda of previous years was not so prominent. While the 1938 text envisaged the reader building his own garage (using asbestos sheets!) the later book assumed the garage to be built with the house. The later book was, in fact, much more concerned with the motor and cycle maintenance and repair that was likely to take place in it. It was simply another reflection of the spirit of self-reliance which guided both publications

New or revamped titles now appeared containing the magic word 'modern'. It echoed the cachet of Modern Jazz, Modern Art, Modern Architecture and Modernism itself. Those who bought these titles were indulging a mid-century taste. Ironically the word Modern had been used earlier in marketing the 'coupon books'. The Modern Home University series had appeared in 1935 and *Modern Cooking Illustrated* in 1938, but the fact probably escaped the attention of the Odhams book department in its post-war form.

One of the 'modern' factors influencing book policy was the increasing, almost insidious influence of radio and television. This showed itself at first in curious ways, for example W.P. (Bill) Matthews, who edited *Modern Home Painting and Decorating* (1954) was described on the title page as "Handyman of BBC radio and television". Soon after this, as we have seen, TV personalities were secured to write titles of their own for Odhams such as *Philip Harben's Cookery Encyclopedia*, or *Labour Saving Gardening* (1956) by the much-loved radio and TV gardener Fred Streeter.

There can be no question which two subjects provided the most titles over the years of Odhams output of books of a reference and 'practical' nature – gardening and knitting/needlework. Both were firmly fixed to a gender specific vision of 'hubby' active in the garden at evening and weekends, and the good wife sitting by the fireside sewing, attended by children looking at books, and occasionally pets. Such scenes were often depicted in frontispiece photographs. In short, these books promoted and reinforced the vision of the 'ideal' middle and lower-middle class family, right down to trying to guide their leisure activities into creative paths. This vision persisted from the early 'thirties until almost at least 1955, during that time, and if we include cookery in the survey, there were at least 25 titles that fell into this frame, in other words more than one book a year, and sometimes some of these were doubtless reprinted. The practical advice given in them, and even the recipes, often varied little, but the books reveal subtle changes in the lives of their target market – from formal borders to the growing of vegetables for the war effort, back to flowers and the rise of the rockery, from the dominance of wool in undergarments and children's clothing to the arrival of manmade fibres, from gas cookers and ranges to the wider ownership of modern electric cookers and refrigerators, the advent of the pressure cookers, etc., etc.

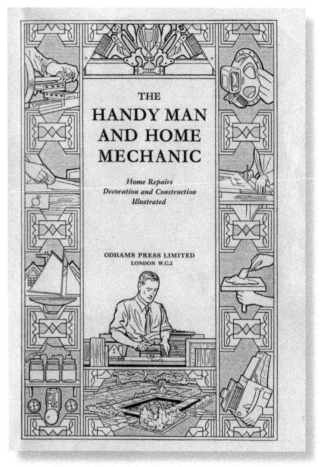

A work of art created from seemingly mundane activities such as measuring wood or mixing mortar.

Practical woman takes to the wheel of the family car. Is this the beginning of the school run? Why else would suburban woman need to drive in 1963?

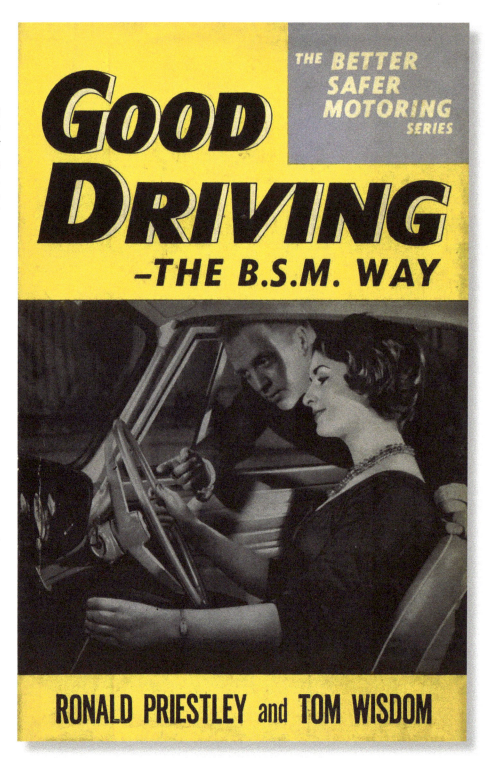

THE BETTER SAFER MOTORING SERIES

GOOD DRIVING
-THE B.S.M. WAY

RONALD PRIESTLEY and TOM WISDOM

TECHNICAL EXPERTISE AND MECHANICAL KNOW-HOW

In addition to the straightforward reference books that the firm brought out, for both adults and children, over the thirty-odd years covered by this survey, it also produced a considerable number of titles intended to give technical expertise and know-how in specialist areas. These areas are extremely varied and diverse, and it is revealing to examine a range of just some of them.

In the absence of any evidence it is as usual a matter of guesswork how Odhams decided that a particular subject was in demand. No definable pattern, either, seems to emerge with the passing of time. The first volume to note is in the 'practical' series, and is *Practical Book-keeping and Accountancy* (1935). It was followed in 1936 by *The Universal Home Lawyer Illustrated*, and this latter title is in the 'home 'series, which always carried a flavour of 'be-your-own'. It could, presumably, be argued that the 'thirties was a decade in which law and accountancy, both traditionally perceived as bookish subjects, had been brought into public prominence.

Keeping fit, physically, mentally and emotionally, remained and, one supposes, continues to be, a popular preoccupation. It spawned a number of titles in the 'thirties – the *Live Successfully* series (13 slim volumes) and at least two *Home Doctors* (1938/9), and a *Medical Guide* (1939).

In an age where accent mattered greatly speaking and writing well was a specialist subject which was partly a social skill, and partly a knowledge of the meaning and function of words. *The Fundamentals of Good English* (1938) and

How to Write and Speak Correctly (1939) both contributed to this skills area, as did, much later *The Art of Conversation* (1953). These are all areas that anyone reading Odhams books might be expected to be interested in.

The range of more 'mechanical' subjects, which involved tools and manual dexterity is fascinating. The opening shot, as it were, was the appearance in 1939 of the *Home Workshop* which served as a kind of introduction to tools and equipment. In 1941 this was followed by *The Handyman Home Mechanic* and *General Engineering Workshop Practice*. The former was part of the DIY ethos of the 'Home' series, whereas the second was more significant since it moved out of the home and into the workplace.

Both the *Home Workshop* and *The Home Mechanic* were unapologetically DIY in approach, albeit this approach is quaintly phrased by modern standards:

> The primary object in producing this volume (Home Workshop) has been not only to inform readers how they can best proceed to carry out a piece of construction or a simple repair about the house, but also…
> …This book is essentially for the reader who enjoys doing things for himself – and to the average man there are few pleasures comparable to that which comes from the completion of a piece of work by his own hands.

This is the DIY background to so many modern successors of this kind of book, but here the explanations are in exquisite English. There is also, as might be expected, the gender distinction which sees working with wood or metal as a male precinct and knitting and sewing as female activities. The educational practice of the time mirrored this, and in many cases would continue to do so until the last quarter of the twentieth century. The **Workshop** was exhaustive in its exploration of what might be done, covering metalworking and the maintenance of motorcycles and cars, in addition to the paperhanging and door-fitting in the house. Neither should it be forgotten that one of the primary stimuli is the desire to save money. The almost complete absence of power-tools in the circumstances is what will immediately strike the modern reader, particularly the younger ones. As if we were not already aware that we were looking back at a very different world, there is also twenty-odd pages of 'Practical Household Precautions against Air-raids (based on the recommendations of the Home Office)'.

One immediate effect of the passage of time is obvious in the very title of *The Home Handyman and Mechanic*. Odhams were here using the word 'mechanic' in an earlier and much wider sense than that of the modern (garage-) mechanic. The word had originally meant 'artisan', one who works with tools, as in the Mechanics Institutes of the nineteenth century. It was with that rather old-fashioned concept that this book was concerned. The editor, James Wheeler, a regular Odhams contributor, had this to say about the aim of the book:

To you, whether you are a seasoned craftsman or just a beginner, this book is dedicated. It is written by practical men in plain and simple language that all can understand…This book will fill your leisure hours with pleasure and profit.

In the straitened circumstances of 1941, the last word especially would have proved an attraction. The range of activities covered is comprehensive, and very similar to that of the **Home Workshop**. The chapter headings are virtually the same, and the advice and instructions given are also the same.

General Engineering Workshop Practice (1941) is a different animal. It is intended not only for the interested amateur, but also for people who have an urgent need to become acquainted with workshop practice. A clue as to who such people might be is to be found in the frontispiece drawing. It is the only drawing of the many technical drawings in this title to show a general view including a human being (a man, not surprisingly), and bears the caption:

A worker in a British munitions factory turning the bases of brass cartridge cases for AA shells.

By the spring of 1941 when this book appeared, large numbers of people, men and women, but increasingly the latter, were being drafted to work in the munitions factories spread across the length and breadth of the British Isles. Given that some, if not many, of those involved would have minimum experience of engineering bench-work the value of a book of this kind is immediately obvious. It is yet another example of the publishers being actively encouraged by the authorities (by the release of paper, perhaps) to produce particular titles. The book has some 500- odd pages of densely packed information about virtually every aspect of engineering workshop practice. It was a breakaway from self-help or early DIY, and into the field of quasi-technical qualifications, and it was to be followed by many other and similar volumes.

In 1943, in the middle of the war, there appeared ***Modern Foundry Practice***. It was one of the few books that Odhams were able to bring out at this juncture. Again, it is fascinating to speculate why. In fact ***Foundry Practice*** did for the making of iron and steel products what the previous book had done for factory engineering, and it gave to those wishing to work in this now vital branch of industry sound practical instruction and advice. Steel was vital to the armaments industry, and home-produced steel even more. Format and presentation were much the same as **Workshop Practice**, with the addition of photographic illustrations which fill with horror those of us whose health and safety sensibilities have been sharpened by the modern obsession with such matters. The incentive to such a publication could very much be seen as contribution to the war effort. Odhams' meagre paper ration may, again, have been increased to facilitate the appearance of the book. (In the same way paper was released to promote the printing of leaflets to be dropped on occupied countries and on Germany itself. With its large capacity plant at Watford Odhams was in the forefront of such activities).

A similar theme is continued by the appearance in 1945 of **The Practical Plumber and Sanitary Engineer.** In April of that year when this book came out the end of the war in Europe was already fact. For more than a year some who had the leisure and incentive to do so had already turned their minds to the question of reconstruction. War damage to the stock of public and private buildings had been enormous, and it was recognised that, amongst other things, there would be a national shortage of builders and plumbers in the early years of the peace. So, once again, Odhams had produced a title which answered a particular social and economic need. For young people looking to train and for ex-servicemen wishing to retrain this would be nearly 400 pages of valuable guidance, particularly as it extended to cover the use of lead in roofing and guttering.

The first full year of peace saw two more apposite titles. The first was a book on **Electric Motors and Generators** (1946). In line with other titles of this kind this book was interested as much in how motors and generators worked, and what they might be used for, as in how they might be serviced and repaired. It was again an introduction for the layman, and a guide for the professional – or, as one of the contributors puts it:

It is obviously to the advantage of the ambitious craftsman in any trade to possess a knowledge of these machines.

Poor diet, cold and damp and emotional stress – all these factors meant that the closing years of the war and the onset of peace had brought ever increasing pressure on the health professions, in particular nursing. The absence of an organised National Health Service also meant that many sick people were being nursed in the home, often by their relatives. Perhaps to answer this situation Odhams moved to reprinting a book originally from 1940-1 **Modern Home Nursing and First Aid** (1946). It was another comprehensive instructional book, covering major and minor ailments, pregnancy, dietary systems, dressings, and, most important, what is required to be a good nurse. With this latter section in mind in particular it is easy to see how the book would also fit in as reading for the woman wishing to go into nursing at this critical moment in health care history.

Domestic and other matters affecting domestic equipment, moved on as the 1940s progressed, as did fittings and fitments of public buildings and public transport. Plastics had begun to replace both artificial substances such as Bakelite and metals in cases when metals as fitments became expensive – or too heavy, or wore out, or rusted. Plastics were durable and could now be coloured and shaped more easily than hitherto. The war years had added a real impetus to the development of synthetic fibres and materials. It was therefore no surprise that Odhams produced in 1947 **Practical Plastics**. A knowledge of how to create and fashion plastics – how to apply them and develop them now became a skill which craftsmen and engineers needed to acquire. In fact the book is much more concerned with the making of resin-based plastics and polymers, and other substances which can loosely be described as plastics, e.g. vinyls, than with the application of these to everyday uses, though it does devote the occasional page or two, and some of the numerous illustrations to 'uses'. Since the materials were relatively new in 1947 space is devoted to the expansion of the plastics industry world-wide. Apart from such non-technical issues the book in the main concerns itself with the chemical composition of plastics, and the creation of machines for finishing and working the end-product. The jacket blurb has this to say:

The information given is primarily intended for those who are already engaged in....the plastics industry.

At the same time the contents have been carefully graded so that the student, or intending student, will have no difficulty in gaining a clear insight into every aspect of plastics manufacture.

Significantly, at the end of the book there is a chapter of half a dozen or so pages on 'Opportunities in the Plastics Industry'.

The Practical Joiner and Carpenter appeared in the same year, but an original 1946 printing had broken the ground. The pressure for housing construction was unrelenting, and it is not at all surprising that this particular title went on being reprinted until well into the 1950s. The subtitle to the 1946 edition underlines the message that the book was not aimed solely at the DIY enthusiast, but instead it was also:

A complete guide to every branch of the trade for all those engaged in the crafts of carpentry and joinery.

The building industry was under intense pressure, and the editor of this book was determined that skill levels were up to standard. There is, however, an open door for school-leavers wishing to enter the trade:

A beginner may be chagrined at his lack of opportunity as he essays his chosen task, and must be prepared for disappointments. But despite the scepticism of many, the desire to achieve and do good is still the mainspring of human endeavour. It is the hallmark of true craftsmanship.

Hardly artisan language, but conveying the message, nevertheless.

Over the next decade at least a dozen titles aimed at the 'handyman', our DIY enthusiast, appeared, covering a range of subjects, from decorating, carpentry to gardening and entertaining.

The next title to fall into our present category was ***Odhams Motor Manual*** (1955, reprinted 1957). There had been previous versions, but that of 1955 comes at the height of the upsurge in private car ownership. Coach and rail holidays were yielding to motoring tours. Significantly it is at this stage (1953) that Odhams produces a road atlas for the British Isles.

The subtitle to the ***Manual*** was ***'Your Car and How it Works'***. General care and maintenance of the family car, and the acquisition of habits of good driving were dealt with by all the editions of the motor manual. Increasingly, however, the drift away from owner repair and servicing to the involvement of the dealer servicing by the garage mechanic began to tell, and the books of this kind became of more use to the trainee motor mechanic in the smaller garages, of which many still existed in the 1950s.

In the end individual manuals for each model meant that even the enthusiast no longer bought the general motor manual. The 1955 edition portrays many operations now shrouded in mystery viz. gudgeon pins, and the dismantling of oil pumps and stripping down of braking systems. The same-day acquisition of replacement parts just was not part of the early 1950s. Yet the *Manual*, edited, as were most of the other motor books, by Staten Abbey, with its 320-odd pages of helpful advice and guidance, was a godsend to the paterfamilias of the time. For him the car was a treasured possession, to be cared for and cleaned regularly. We are still in the age where suburbanites rarely took the car to work, but used it for weekend pleasure.

The manuals were on the edge of professional activity, on the dividing line between owner care and garage mechanic. Between 1955 and 1957 there appeared the third edition of *General Automobile Engineering*. This title, even in its earlier editions had cast a completely different perspective on the subject of car care. As suggested by the word engineering, this was a book for the trade. It aimed to be –

A comprehensive guide for everyone connected with the automobile industry, with special sections on maintenance, overhaul and repair. Each chapter has been contributed from practical experience by a specialist in the trade.

Its 500-odd pages contained all the detail of the *Manual*, and more. The layout, it said:

has been so planned that it is suitable not only for the experienced engineer and mechanic, but also for students and apprentices...

Yet, even as the book came out, the publishers realised with desperation that the subject was changing and developing so rapidly that each edition was outdated as soon as it appeared. They were going to have to react in a different way, as we shall see below.

The next title to fall partly in the professional and partly in the amateur mould was *Radio, TV and Electrical Repairs* (1948). In some ways it was a logical successor to *Electric Motors and Generators*, for here was a title mostly to do with the domestic applications of electric power, specifically to do with radio and the burgeoning television, but also about electrical appliances in general. Developments in all these fields were moving often at a startling pace, and it is no surprise that the book went to three editions, and eight or nine reprints. The aim, as stated in the foreword to the third edition, was to give a grounding in the three areas, both to the layman and to the apprentice or newcomer to the profession of radio/TV engineer and repairman. This edition had been updated to allow for the inclusion of FM radio and VHF in television, but between 1948 and the early 1960s the world of TV and radio had changed dramatically, bringing into the language terms such as 'hi-fi', stereo, record-player.

By 1960 the comprehensive style of the book, an all inclusive compendium, was becoming unpopular, and it is not surprising to see that the dust-jacket to the third edition carried advertisements for three separate, shorter books on Hi-fi, FM radio and TV servicing. They are further described as 'handbooks'.

As far as cars were concerned Odhams had settled upon a similar solution. They updated the *Manual* to include the later models and American cars, but realised at the same time that the day of the general book had gone, and the future was the workshop manual devoted to each model. By 1958 Odhams had already become involved in publishing such books. *The Ford Popular Handbook* came out in that year, to be followed by a selection of companion volumes, mostly for the lower and middle market models. The art of good driving was also given new treatment, this

PLASTICS IN THE HOME

A profusion of plastics products for domestic and personal use is here shown to colourful advantage. Many of the items are easily recognizable as being made from plastics, but one may fail to notice that such things as the top of the occasional table, the umbrella handle, necklace and bracelets, wall ornament, curtains and even curtain runner are made from plastics materials. Most shades of colour are possible and coloration is permanent.

Practical Plastics

Published in 1947, this instructional book about the manufacture of polymer plastics created a relationship bewteen this new technology and its consumer.

time outside the compendium volume framework. ***Good Driving*** appeared as a slim pocket volume produced in conjunction with the British School of Motoring. It came out in 1963, and was immediately so popular that it went into six reprints over the next eighteen months. It is short, succinct and well illustrated using traffic layouts with model cars. Although women were shown driving, or at least learning to drive – it was not assumed they would in any way actually work on the car, even though many had in fact trained in this in the ATS during the war and subsequently.

Times have changed. The ***Manual*** had started in 1949, and the 1955 reprint still contained a chapter 'On the Road, a Touring Holiday' – by 1957 this was already taken for granted, and had been omitted.

In the early 1960s Odhams turned their attention to another activity which was becoming a leisure pastime, and had always been a professional business – photography. Two editions of ***Odhams Manual of Photography*** were produced at the beginning of the decade, the second an update of the first. This was another rapidly changing field. Both camera design, size and processing were advancing, as more and more people were taking holiday 'snaps', as they were still called, and increasingly in colour. Professional skills, however, were dealt with by ***Odhams Practical Photography and Film-making*** (1964). This title envisaged studio work, outdoor photography, and, as a new arrival, filming with hand-held cameras for later viewing at home. It was the stage immediately before the arrival of video. In addition the book covered the making of studio feature films and documentaries, and techniques such as the addition of sound, and questions of lighting, etc. It stood slightly to one side of the Odhams' mainstream in that it was a translation of a French original. Many of the illustrated examples are French, though in 1964 this had a certain cachet. It obviously pre-dates digital photography. Though many of the pages are devoted to now outdated cameras, the techniques and the composition and lighting are still applicable. The 1960s were significant years in the popularisation of 'art photography', as it came to be known, and this title was very much of its time. It is the sort of book anyone moving into the field, either professionally or as a hobby, would be likely to acquire.

Finally, it is difficult not to include here, as a postscript, one more title which is almost Odhams presenting itself. *Practical Printing and Binding* appeared in the early autumn of 1946. The print and publishing trades had both suffered during the war. The suffering had taken two forms – the contraction of the workforce as men were drafted to the forces or defence work, and as women took jobs in munition factories, or the health and emergency services. This situation was reflected in equal measure in the papermaking trade, exacerbated by the shortage of the materials needed to produce paper of even the war economy standard. There was also the question of loss of stock due to enemy action. Many printing firms had lost machinery and premises as a result of air-raids, both in the capital and the provinces.

1946 was thus the beginning of reconstruction for printing, publishing and papermaking. A book, therefore, which gave an introduction to the processes and the skills needed in these trades was valuable as a recruitment and retraining weapon. *Practical Printing and Binding* did just that in the usual Odhams manner, comprehensive, detailed, and just a little old-fashioned. It covered all aspects of the trades in its nearly 450 pages, was extremely well illustrated, and left few questions unanswered, priding itself on including the latest developments. It made great play in the text of the need for cooperation within and between the various trades involved – something that the experience of the war had brought home to all. If we recall the printing and publishing of pamphlets and propaganda leaflets undertaken by Odhams, then we can appreciate the claim made by the foreword to this title that:

Printing touches every aspect of the life of the Nation...

As to directing the text to a particular reader or market, the foreword goes on:

The aim has been to give, in a single volume,
expert practical instruction in every branch
of printing, so that apprentices, learners,
and craftsmen generally may increase their
knowledge of the latest methods employed.

- and if the reading of the book brought Odhams itself more post-war recruits then so much the better!

Another curious offshoot of this effort to equip the interested learner with technical and professional expertise was the appearance in 1961 of a volume on *Railway Operating Practice*. The timing was not as unexplained as it might seem. British Railways, as it then was, was creaking at the joints to catch up with the modern world, with a map of lines still based on a world with few cars and buses, largely pre-war rolling-stock, largely still steam-powered, virtually no electric signalling, and so forth. It could well be that impending modernisation, and a greater degree of capitalisation forecast a need for more and newly trained staff. It is equally likely that expanding rail operation in the Commonwealth was also a motive.

The 30's fascination with speed and streamlining carried over into the post-war world.

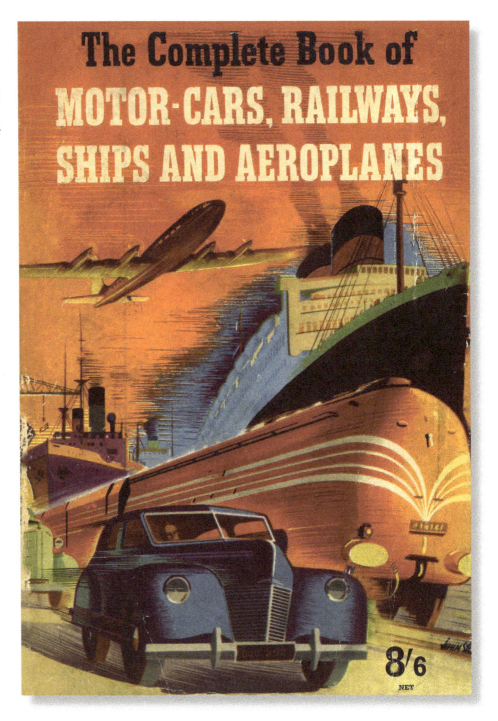

The Complete Book of
MOTOR-CARS, RAILWAYS, SHIPS AND AEROPLANES

8/6
NET

THE WORLD OF MACHINES

It is a well-known perception of the 1920s and 1930s that this was a period when the popular imagination was obsessed with machines and the speed with which they could or might be able to travel. As examples one could quote dirigibles (until some well-documented disasters), the Schneider Trophy, the Blue Riband of the Atlantic, world land-speed records, records on water, fastest express locomotive, etc, etc. Then came the Second World War, which contrasted with the first European conflict by being total and highly mechanised, the spin-off from which, as often happens, fuelled increased mechanisation in civilian life.

The implication of these factors, as far as book publishing was concerned was the making available of an avid readership for titles concerned with the world of machines, particularly later with those which increased our ability to travel farther and faster. Odhams, however, began by looking at the static machine, rather than transport. The book concerned was *How it Works and How it's Done* (1939). This was, if one may use the phrase, a typical pre-war Odhams book, in the larger format with dark red/ maroon boards, with some 500-odd pages, and lavishly illustrated. Significantly for later titles the frontispiece shows many streamlined (a word then much in vogue) forms of transport. The seventeen chapters range from how modern drainage works to the workings of a diesel engine, and from television to the functioning of a trolleybus, an autogyro and a harvester. As the book title suggests it is not merely about the working principles of the machines described, but also about their operation. The words 'wonder' and 'wonderful' are fairly frequently used in the text, and thus tilt the presentation of the book away from the educational and more towards 'read and be surprised/ entertained'. There is, therefore, a slight leaning towards the younger reader. Nevertheless, the explanations in the text are quite frequently of a complex nature and in no way patronising in tone.

By the time the Second World War came to an end books from Odhams, as we have noted in other chapters, began to acquire a different and more 'modern' shape indeed as had many of the technological objects reviewed in the pre-war book. Based on the experience of the books on the armed services, the post-war books were slimmer, about half the length, and generally speaking the dark red boards alternated with blue boards, dust-jackets and endpapers with artwork.

The first of these to appear, at the very beginning of 1946 was *Everyday Things and their Story*. There was a subtitle which ran 'the romantic (sic) story of modern industry and how it supplies our needs'. With some exceptions the contents were much concerned with the mechanised production of 'everyday things' – needles, matches, coins, false teeth, etc. Whether the story was in every case 'romantic' was down to the perception of the reader – in most cases interest and curiosity were satisfied, 'romance' was another matter.

Within three months there appeared a reprint of a title which had first seen the light of day somewhat earlier, and had now come round to a reprint, but without any apparent or declared updating. The book concerned was *Triumphs of Engineering* (1946) which dealt with a number of engineering projects, most of them very well-known, which involved bridging, tunnelling or canalising, using, of course, machines. As the book's subtitle puts it – 'Man overcoming nature'. It was the same format as **Everyday Things**, with over 200 illustrations – photographs and drawings.

This concentration on the role of machines had also been evident in **The General Engineering Workshop** (1941) and **Miracles of Invention and Discovery** (1945), both of them cast rather more in the pre-war mould. As nearly all of the texts discussed so far were anonymously authored they give the impression of being commissioned directly by the publishers, which in its turn reinforces the notion of deliberate but unelaborated policy.

One tends to forget, from the perspective of post-industrial Britain, the degree to which the prosperity of the country had been heavily dependent on engineering and machinery. The positive, progressivist attitude of all the titles so far discussed would in this way have a salutary impact on a young readership. Becoming an apprentice in the engineering industry was still, in post-war Britain, a step worth taking.

From the closing years of the 1930s onwards Odhams had been catering for the growing interest in descriptions of the workings of means of transport, an interest, as we have seen, in 'streamlining' and speed. **Railways, Ships and Planes Illustrated** (1946 reprint) was typical in this respect. It was a precursor of the car/bus/train/plane/ship books which were to follow in the 1950s and 1960s. **Railways, Ships** etc was produced in the standard post-war format for this type of book, bound in blue boards and with a dust-jacket. The end-papers were a stylised, repeated 'transport' pattern. It was 300-odd pages in length, including about the same number of illustrations. It was a hallmark Odhams book of this vintage.

In 1950 there followed **The Wonderful Story of the Sea** this also partly dealt with the mechanised world, but it was combined with a historical perspective stretching back to the days of sail and (briefly) beyond. Once this short introduction was past the book became a celebration of the sea as a travel medium and of what was still seen as Britain's role as a leading maritime power. The country was, in fact on the brink of slipping from this position.

This was a title which received more than the standard format. It was rather going towards the coffee table size. There was an identifiable, and highly qualified, 'advisory editor'. In line with other volumes in this format the end-papers were plain. It was almost the last such volume, celebrating as it did a Britain that was rapidly disappearing. Subsequent books on mechanisation became much more specialised and applied.

In the course of the 1950s the term 'transport enthusiast' had come into currency to describe those readers who had developed an 'observer' interest in all forms of mechanical transport. Odhams had in their magazine portfolio a periodical called **Modern Transport** read by both those working in the industry and enthusiasts. At the end of the decade Odhams began to produce a series of large format books for older children under the imprint Swift Picture Books, a series which Odhams appear to have taken over from Hulton Press when they acquired them in 1959. There were some fifteen titles in all ranging from predictable subjects such as ballet to the Wild West, and from Horses and Ponies to British military uniforms. At least half the series, however, fell within the remit of this section since they were about machines e.g. **Cars of the World, Trains of the World, Ships, Buses, Coaches and Lorries**. These consisted of brief explanatory captions to 60 pages of mostly photographic images from a variety of trade sources and collections. As they stood they were prized as much by the enthusiast as by older children to whom they may have come as gifts. Compared with any earlier books on railways, ships and planes these early 60s titles reflected a different world, and a different way of looking at machines, and, as might be expected, gave greater emphasis to road transport. This was made necessary by the phenomenal growth in car ownership. In 1939 there were only 2 million private cars in the UK. By 1950 this figure had doubled and in 1951 14% of the population had access to a car, but ownership really escalated in the decade that followed. Publication of the series continued until 1962. There were, naturally many competing titles from other sources, and Odhams joined the considerable number of publishers indulging this new taste for vintage images, partly inspired by and partly reflected by such popular films as **Genevieve** (1953) – about the London to Brighton vintage car run. Although the term was not actually current at the time we are reaching the stage when certain models and designs could be regarded as 'iconic'. Possibly with this in mind Odhams moved to a fresh imprint and a new 'landscape' picture book format. The imprint was Longacre Press, derived from the site of Odhams London offices. The titles began to appear in 1962 and went on to 1963. They consisted of **The Longacre Book of Cars** and went on to cover ships, aircraft and trains – four books in all. As has been hinted, they contrasted markedly with the Swift picture books in containing not photographic images, but handsomely executed hand drawings in colour of the relevant car, ship, train or 'plane. They also contained black and white line drawings and quarter pages of several hundred words of simple explanatory text. The illustrations frequently showed what are now and were even then regarded as 'classic' models, and were often of a sufficiently high quality to make some of them frameable. Where this sort of disfiguration did not

take place some children often retained one or more of these titles well into adulthood. Nor has their appeal been diminished, as our love-affair with modes of transport has continued into the present century.

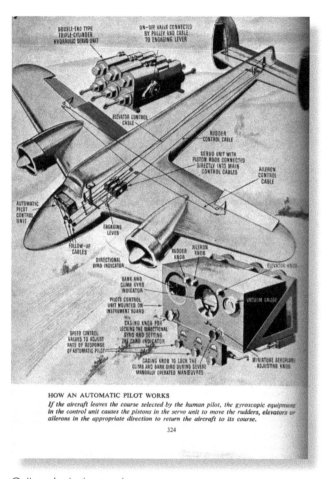

HOW AN AUTOMATIC PILOT WORKS
If the aircraft leaves the course selected by the human pilot, the gyroscopic equipment in the control unit causes the pistons in the servo unit to move the rudders, elevators or ailerons in the appropriate direction to return the aircraft to its course.

324

Odham's desire to show how even quite complex things work is never better illustrated than here.

When it came to
explaining the countryside
to suburbanites the
book illustrations were,
themselves, works of art.
In this instance a painting
by S.R. Badmin.

UPPER SLAUGHTER, COTSWOLDS

*The character of the Cotswold scene is distinctive and individual; it arises mainly from the use of locally
quarried limestone for building purposes. Here is shown the village of Upper Slaughter, its Cotswold
character unmistakable in stone cottages and farmsteads, walls instead of hedges, and the stone church.
The latter was built during the medieval woollen boom when the Wold was very prosperous.*

NATURE, COUNTRYSIDE, AND COUNTRY MATTERS

Over the period covered by this book Odhams produced more than thirty titles that fall into this category, though a fair proportion of them were part of a series on various aspects of the countryside.

There are identifiably distinct phases in the output of these titles, and the titles themselves divide into two related groups.

One of the direct outcomes of the suburbanisation of Britain, under way since the last decade of the nineteenth century, was that more and more former city dwellers found themselves in closer touch than ever with wild life and the natural world. One of the sales lines of Metroland, after all, was that moving there was like going out into the open air. Metroland country walk books had been appearing since 1905 and the London Passenger Transport Board, and its successor London Transport, both continued to publish them. The rapid increase in private car ownership, and improvements in interurban and rural public transport, already under way during the 'thirties and accelerating again in the 1950s, meant that all classes of urban and suburban dwellers made more frequent forays into the countryside. The young had begun this trend in the pre-war decade as they followed the fashionable crazes of hiking and cycling. The scout and guide movement, with its predominantly rural ethos, was also at its height at this time, sponsored by such prominent figures as the then Prince of Wales. Thus, all in all, the countryside, including everything that the term embraced, was a magnet for those who did not work in it. Sadly, for those who did work

in it, farming at this period was in the doldrums and was not to recover until under pressure in the war years, and the need to keep the nation fed. So interest was less in the country way of life (which, ironically, many country dwellers were seeking to escape) and centred more on topography, vernacular architecture, and flora and fauna, although rural crafts were occasionally touched upon. The first 'phase' of Odhams countryside books opened with *Britain's Wonderland of Nature* (1934), the titling of which is in line with other informative 'wonder' volumes of the 1930s and 1940s, then followed *Lovely Britain* (1939), planned before the outbreak of war, *Romantic Britain* (1940), *The Wonders of Nature* (1944), *Nature Through the Year* (1946), *Birds, Trees and Flowers Illustrated* (1947) and *The Nature Lover's Companion* (1949). The trauma of the war undoubtedly turned the mind to the simple continuity visible in nature, and in the 1940's, and for some time afterwards, being a 'nature lover' had cosy and positive connotations. From the point of view of the publisher (and the Ministry of Information) there was also the wider point of reminding the readership of the beauties of the country they were fighting for. In another medium the parallel is with Frank Newbould's civilian war posters.

None of these volumes on Britain's natural world was in any way academic or specialist, all were lavishly illustrated, the quality of the reproductions improving as the years went by. They are all written in an unpatronising tone which the layman would readily accept and understand. Other branches of the media reflected this public interest in wildlife, both British and exotic. Certainly, in the period after the war personalities such as Ludwig Koch, Armand and Michaela Denis, George Cansdale and Brian Veasey-Fitzgerald with their radio and TV programmes, helped to foster public interest and enthusiasm. Kenneth Richmond, writing **Birds in Britain** as late as 1962, does so with thoroughness when dealing with identification, habitat and behaviour, but he also writes with humour and anecdote in a way that makes the book very readable – though, like some of its Odhams predecessors, it is pre-eminently a book for the bookshelf, and not the sort of thing to be slipped into the pocket or rucksack for a walk in the country. If, as Richmond wrote, the British might by 1962 be perceived as a nation of bird-watchers, then most of the books listed earlier had reflected and fostered this public preoccupation.

Lovely Britain and **Romantic Britain** (with an introduction by Tom Stephenson, the popular countryside 'right-to-roam' campaigner) were possibly produced before Odhams' already rationed allocation of paper was even more drastically reduced. Nevertheless, as pointed out above, both books were in line with the current official desire to encourage the British people to value, cherish and defend the land they lived in. It was very much a question of tradition and heritage though in themselves these aspects were not actual subject matter until **The British Heritage** (1948) and **Historic Britain** (late 1950's), long after the period of subtle political direction.

In the third decade of the twentieth century Britain had a more mobile population than possibly ever before, the working classes seeking employment away from their home area, and the middle classes increasingly motoring for pleasure. The fourth decade, with the war, served only to accelerate social mobility. Men, and some women, went to military camps in distant parts of Britain. First children, and then whole families were evacuated to avoid the bombing and the threatened invasion. A few years after the war, as the economy began to pick up, car ownership again slowly increased. More importantly, large sections of the community began once more to take an annual holiday, mostly to begin with travelling on the newly nationalised and still shaky rail system, but increasingly also by car and coach. This time was the start of the golden age of the motor coach. More and more people, especially the elderly and the middle aged were taking their annual holiday in the form of a coach tour. If we examine the itineraries of these tours then the titles of Odhams second phase and second group of countryside books explain themselves.

The format of the books involved is in itself interesting. The phase began with what might be called an 'orthodox' Odhams book, from the point of view of size and presentation – this was **The English Counties Illustrated** (1948). It was a blend of informative and descriptive text with plentiful illustrations, in the main black and white photographs. It must have proved popular because it went into reprints, including an updated version in 1958. The updating included fresh illustrations.

The twin series which this book set going looks, in retrospect, like an album of souvenir photographs from a number of coach tours. In size the titles concerned were 10"x 7" with olive green binding and multicoloured photographic dust jackets. They were all some 125-130 pages long with 120 of these illustrations and some explanatory and introductory text and a minimal index. The standard of the photographic images was for the period at times relatively high. They were in the main standard postcard views of already well known beauty spots. The two volumes which began this double mini series were **Devon and**

Cornwall in Pictures and **English Cathedrals and Abbeys Illustrated** both of which appeared in 1950. In all the series went on for seven years, ending with **North Wales in Pictures.**

Topographic and regional village-orientated books were described as 'in pictures' whereas architectural monuments were 'illustrated'. The areas chosen for 'in pictures' were fairly universally recognised as 'picturesque': the Scottish countryside, the Home Counties (shades of Greenline coaches), the lake district, rural London, the Highlands, English villages, Yorkshire, the Shakespeare country, North Wales, Historic towns of England, and so forth. With few exceptions they are all part of the coach tour scene. It is noticeable that by no means all the illustrations are contemporary with the books, and it was often necessary in the introduction to make some explanation of the damage done by bombing, so that there is unavoidably a backward looking slant given to the whole volume.

The 'illustrated' books also chose by and large predictable subjects – cathedrals and abbeys, castles and manor houses, English inns, royal homes. At that stage not all of these last had been opened to the public, and then often only partially. Thus for those who visited the grounds only, and for many others, the book was the only chance they had to see the interiors. At the time Britain was maybe not nearly as egalitarian as now and deference still played a significant part in public attitudes. Public figures of all kinds commanded a respect which is now only dreamt of.

Odhams sought to give the 'illustrated' and 'in pictures' books status and extra respectability by engaging notable public figures to contribute forewords and introductions. To this end they enrolled the services of four members of the House of Lords: Lord Latham; Lord Harlech (formerly Ormsby-Gore, Minister of Works in

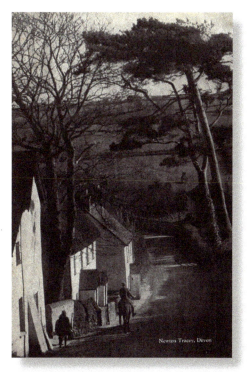

Publications such as this, provided regular work for the emerging profession of photography.

the wartime government); the Earl of Harewood, and Sir Norman Birkett QC. Other public figures involved in this way were A L Rowse; Brian Vesey-Fitzgerald; and Sir William Beach Thomas. Not surprisingly the North Wales book was sponsored by Lady Megan Lloyd-George. All these 'names' were intended to give a stamp of authority and approval to the pictures presented.

It could be said with some certainty that British farming benefitted from the war years and the period of austerity that followed them. Production rose and the face of the countryside changed. The pace of agricultural mechanisation quickened in the face of the threat of imminent national starvation. The now almost hackneyed 'Dig for Victory' campaign raised public awareness of the land as a valuable resource. Thousands of Land Army women were introduced to the arduous nature of work on the farm. School age children too were brought face to face with the life of rural communities.

Nevertheless, a short time after the war there still remained a gulf of understanding between town and country. Farmers viewed townspeople with suspicion and even hostility, and townspeople, especially away from the smaller market towns and in the city and metropolitan areas, saw the countryside as picturesque, good for picnics, quaintly backward and, occasionally, somewhere quiet for retirement. Britain was not alone in having this polarisation of attitudes. It was shared by other European and North American economies at the time, and expressed in terms like 'rustics' and 'townees', 'hicks' and 'city slickers'.

As evidence of how 'directed' the British media still were long after the demise of the Ministry of Information we may take two titles which appeared at the start of a decade when a raft of Odhams country books came out.

> *It is not, I think, very difficult to appreciate scenery. It is easy enough to write a descriptive and topographical account of certain features of the British countryside. You need only the detached view of the connoisseur. But that is less than half the picture. The British rural scene was made with hands and, therefore, if the canvas is to be complete, the painter must be included in the picture.*

This corrective remark is taken from Brian Vesey-Fitzgerald's introduction to **The Country Lover's Companion** (1950), a book which presented itself, on the title page as 'The wayfarer's guide to the varied scenery of Britain and the people who live and work in the countryside'.

Other media attempts to bring the layman to a fuller understanding of how the countryman

(farmer, farm-worker, craftsman) lives included a highly popular radio and TV programme **Country Magazine** (cf. present day **Countryfile**), hosted by the popular Ralph Wightman. In the linguistically anodyne corridors of the BBC it was refreshing to hear a real range of regional accents. Normally these were reserved for comedy programmes. It could be argued that at the time Wightman was doing for the discussion of country matters what John Arlott was doing for cricket. In 1950 Odhams produced a digest of the programme in book form with the title **Country Magazine**. In the foreword Donald McCulloch (of radio Brains Trust fame) wrote the following about the origins of the programme **Country Magazine**:

> *The aim was to create a better team spirit between people working in factories and people working in fields. We wanted to remind people living under great strain in the cities that the people in the country were doing their best to help.*

That was in 1942 – the third year of the war. A G Street, himself a writer on farming, broadcaster and personality, had this to say in his introduction about the radio programme which formed the background of the book:

> *There are several reasons for its continuous success over seven years. One is because there was no attempt at cleverness, no sign of stunting. Another is because this programme played no politics. Another because Country Magazine painted in sound a faithful picture of its subject, giving farming its proper representation, but always admitting that there were other aspects of country life.*

Street's remark about politics is nevertheless somewhat ingenuous. In the narrow, party sense of course neither the radio nor the book version was in any way partisan, but they played a part in a wider social directive which both the BBC and apparently Odhams had developed for themselves since the end of the war.

Farming, of course, as Street rightly points out, is only one aspect of life in the country. Nevertheless, because Odhams were interested in exploring how people do their jobs, they were happy to engage James Gunston, who was later to write **Understanding the Countryside** (1962); to write **Farming, Learning and Earning** (1958). This was a basic survey of what was needed by those who wanted a career in farming. It reflected two very interesting aspects of the late 'fifties, namely that farming was a career that could be taken up by people who had virtually no previous experience, but also that there were empty farms going begging.

The sense of 'team' referred to by McCulloch above was reflected in **The Secrets of Other Peoples' Jobs** (1944) and **How the Other Man Lives** (1949). Both books tried to bring together all kinds of work, urban and rural, in an overall picture. Thus they selected a wide variety of occupations, and looked either at groups or individuals in some detail. The wartime ethos which gave rise to both these books extended, in Odhams eyes, well on into the increasingly affluent 'fifties. In the final analysis Odhams country books came to an end simultaneously with an era in which attitudes to the British countryside contained few, if any, references to the 'environment', 'ecology' or 'organic', an era in which the intensive use of chemicals in farming was accepted practice. Neither had the term 'endangered species' yet become current.

All of these issues are illustrated by one of Odhams final ventures into this area **Understanding the Countryside**. As we have seen already, the editor was again John Gunston, though this was a much less didactic exercise than the previous title. Gunston was not born into farming, and

that may account for the curiously mixed tone of this second book. He approached farming from outside, and then was active mainly in small-holding. 'Understandiing' in the title suggests that the aim was to inform those (town-dwellers) who might not appreciate or comprehend country matters. They would have to want to do this pretty badly, because the style of the book is alternately jingoistic, patronising, and genuinely informative, with very slight touches of humour. Much of the book is technical, for example the sections on farming, fishing, and on drainage and irrigation, and would only be taken in in detail by the reader really keen on the subject. The book is, however, prevented from becoming an instructional manual by culling basic information from the subject matter of other previous Odhams books, and redressing it. Britain's towns and villages had already been extensively covered by other titles, but they have a chapter devoted to them here, as do natural history, peoples and landscape. There are numerous illustrations, most of them new black and white photographs, and fourteen colour plates.

There is a sense in which the book sums up Odhams attitude to country matters as a subject, and it does so just at the end of an era in rural Britain, which was on the verge of a new period of intensive farming, pesticides, motorways, pylons and dormitory villages. The picture it transmits is hard to grasp in our own age of green issues, global warming, and threats to wild life. Some matters seem to have come full circle. We find Gunston, for example, advocating coniferisation in forestry, only shortly before others are sounding alarm bells on the same topic. The war, which caused such great changes in British agriculture, and partly set a pattern, is socially significant enough to warrant a chapter of its own in this survey.

Published prior to WWII this would have been the first glimpse many Britons would have of nations and peoples outside the British Isles.

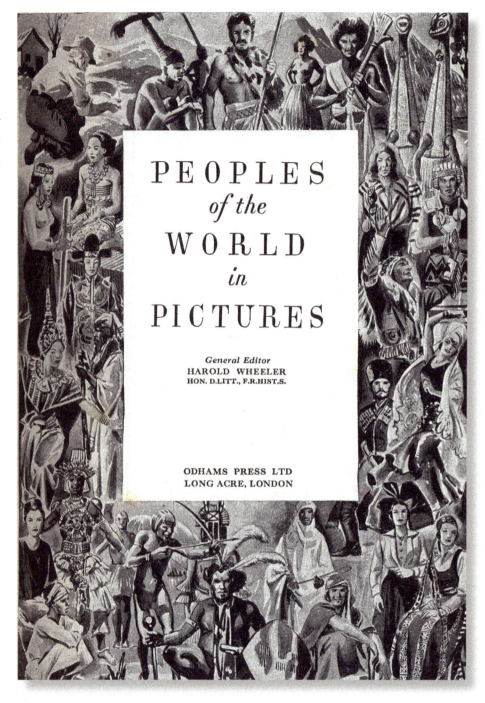

PEOPLES
of the
WORLD
in
PICTURES

General Editor
HAROLD WHEELER
HON. D.LITT., F.R.HIST.S.

ODHAMS PRESS LTD
LONG ACRE, LONDON

THE WIDER WORLD

As we have seen above Odhams were conscious of the demand for pictorial records of the British countryside, and to a lesser extent of those who lived and worked there. But they were also keenly aware of the potential for titles which dealt with more exotic far-away places – and for the period we are examining for most readers these places were to remain distant and exotic, reachable only through film, radio, TV – and books.

In 1934 appeared the ambitiously titled **Story of the World in Pictures**. It is basically a picture book with around one thousand photographic (sepia) images in 600-odd pages. Text is minimal, reduced on average to three-line captions. It is the aim of the book to show the alien, curious and exotic world of faraway. There is a two-page preface and a page or so introduction to each of the chapters or sections. Two quotations from the preface are sufficient to demonstrate the aim of the book:

Our forefathers listened breathless to travellers' tales of men with but a single eye in the middle of the forehead, of fire-breathing basilisks, of mermaid sirens. We can see here more and greater wonders still, the wonders of truth even stranger than fiction from real countries quite as romantic as those 'fabled isles' of ancient story…

…Here are priceless photographs, to take which men have risked their lives, and spent their fortunes. The world's treasuries of wonders have been ransacked for them.

Yet, despite the 'wonder' which the editors think the book will call forth, there is a strong didactic tone to the chapter headings. A brief selection of these will suffice to illustrate this point:

How Man feeds himself

The scientific production of food

What Man wears

How Man shelters himself

Towns and Cities

What Man is building

Nature versus Man

Man versus Nature

Religions of the world

Because the book needs to be both didactic and universal in its coverage it must needs look at not only the wonders, but the way the Western, mechanised world behaves in the first half of the twentieth century.

It is, of course, essentially an imperialist, Eurocentric view of the world, with its attitude to the peoples of Africa and Asia as 'natives', and the use of the terms 'darkie' and 'negro' referring to North America.

Four years later a second, similar book appeared **Peoples of the World in Pictures** (1938). This was less didactic, and was more interested in exploring the world's ethnic variety. The chapter divisions are not thematic, but arranged continent by continent, area by area. In a way the brief initial chapter which acts as a preface tackles the problem of competing media as far as this kind of subject is concerned. If the first book was unaware of this competition the second book is very conscious of it:

If it were possible for a pageant of the world's peoples

to be shown on the silver screen of your nearest cinema, and each individual took no more than a second to play his part, the performances would go on night and day without cessation for over sixty years. Of the 2,000,000,000 men women and children in the grand march past, the majority would be of the white race, followed by members of the yellow, brown, black and red races in decreasing but amazing numbers. This is the book of the procession – a tremendous theme, and surely the most fascinating of all the many matters with which humanity concerns itself. Fortunately the reader is neither limited to a momentary glance, nor committed to an overwhelming cast. He has leisure and selection on his side; can stop and appreciate 'stills' of representative actors and actresses. That is why the printed page triumphs over the fleeting value of the cinema. The one is permanent, the other but the reflection of passing shadows.

The text which accompanies the 1,000-odd photographic images is less concerned with reflecting wonder at the exotic than, as the book's title suggests, with describing something of the way of life of the people in the photos. This is done quite conscientiously, but in an unconsciously racist way. As an example the Chinese (varied as they are ethnically) are treated to a scant few lines of summary judgement:

The Chinese are a sedentary race, with none of the Western passion for exercise. Their virtues are patience and perseverance, an immense aptitude for work and an ability to live comfortably in any clime and in surroundings devoid of any hint of comfort. They have a keen sense of humour, but no sense of time.

- there speaks, one suspects, the colonial administrator, not the ethnographer.

When all is considered this is an informative book, has acceptable flashes of insight and humour, and gives at least a taster to those who want to appreciate different cultures in different parts of the world. The imperialist overtones are quite predictable, and they moulded public thinking until the population movements and upheavals of the Second World War.

Like its predecessor **Peoples of the World** is a library shelf book, large in format, well bound and generally a weighty volume. It is hard to envisage the marketing and purchasers of these large books. One can only consider them presentation items, as presents or prizes. It may even be that in a pre-TV age those who bought the book felt that no home should be without such an informative and visually rewarding publication. We may now never know as the generation who made, sold and bought them is sadly passing away.

In the same year, 1938, there appeared another large format, copiously illustrated book comparable with the two preceding ones. On this occasion it was devoted to one area of the empire – southern Africa. **A Pictorial History of South Africa** is in fact an almost academic history of a part of the Empire whose history is both very complex and full of conflicts of various kinds. The book tracks the history of strife between the various colonial powers, between different groups of settlers, and between settlers and indigenous peoples. Its remit is in fact most of British Africa, including the mandated territories which had been German colonies prior to 1916. It has to be remembered here that the political situation in South Africa in the year in which the book appeared was far from being settled. Nevertheless it was a part of the Empire which still had a powerful attraction for emigrants from Britain. Of all the dominions it was the one most intriguing to a British readership – the Boer War was after all only just over a generation away. The anonymous author of the text has worked wonders in achieving a balanced picture. The market for such a well-produced shelf book was obviously more restricted than for the first two books in this section, yet to those who read it it opened up Africa in a way no film could have done. The copy in my own library was given as a Christmas present in 1941.

Between 1937 and 1958, including the war years, Odhams produced and subsequently reprinted two very different 'world' books. Different, that is, one from the other. Yet both had similar titles and both were focussed on the wider world. The first was **Marvels of the Modern World**. Handsomely bound, lavishly illustrated, and in large book format this volume is not about the natural world. The clue to the contents is in the word 'modern'. The book in fact deals in some detail with engineering and technical achievements in all parts of the world, from planes, ships and trains to radio-telegraphy and ferro-concrete. It really was a splendid gift for the younger reader, although one has no way of telling how, and to whom marketing was directed. Technology develops, however, and the 1946 reprints and later editions were already going out into a different world, different even from 1941.

The world, however continued to be presented on the basis of the pre-war vision. One title which had first come out in the late 1930s was issued again in 1941, just prior to strict paper rationing, and resurfaced in 1946 after the war. It was Hendrik van Loon's **The Home of Mankind**. In its medium format and 500-odd pages it trod ground covered by all the previously discussed books, barring the more technologically orientated **Marvels of the Modern World**. Van Loon's book was concerned with man and environment, civilisations in different surroundings. The writer was a Dutch-American historian and award-winning children's writer. Van Loon died in 1944, and later editions of his work were updated by his sons. To a certain extent a book of this nature might seem escapist, appearing as it did at a time when conflict had

engulfed large areas of the Northern Hemisphere, It may equally, though, have been reassuring in so far as it represented a vision of progress and continuity. Because the book seemed to be sailing on a different sea from most of its readers it was felt necessary to append a publisher's note which it is worth reproducing in full, since it is only brief.

Since Dr van Loon wrote his geography of the world international events have cause sudden and violent changes in certain national boundaries. In many European countries native forms of government are temporarily eclipsed, and conditions of life in these lands are hidden from observers in Great Britain and America.

It has seemed well not to apply any process of revision to the geographical and political statements contained in this book. The present cloud which lies over Europe is no more than transient, and with its passing Dr van Loon's account will be substantially correct again.

The book was out of line with other Odhams books in that even at this stage it was published in collaboration with Harraps, and both publishers seemed to regard their note as a kind of disclaimer. The text and presentation of the book were somewhat eccentric. It was hand illustrated in a sketchy and almost cartoon-like way – yet it is extraordinarily effective. Its thinking is complex and adult, and its end-views are reasonably balanced, yet its audience was almost certainly adolescents. At times it verges on the modern fashion for Horrible Histories, at others it is serious meat for the teen-age reader to get his or her teeth into. Best summed up, perhaps, by what the author himself says at the beginning of the book:

Man comes first in this Geography.
His physical environment and background come next.
The rest is given whatever space remains.

Significantly, more pages are devoted to Europe – 200 pages out of 500, than to other continents, and of the remaining 300, 100 are given over to general introduction. Certainly, this view of Planet Earth is a Eurocentric one, yet reflecting largely the more enlightened opinions of the interwar years. The puzzle remains: why did this particular title go on being brought out across the years of war and beyond?

In 1943 what might be called by comparison the Empire-centric view was fostered by the appearance of *The Story of the British Empire in Pictures*. At the particular juncture in the conflict at which it appeared it achieved a double purpose – first to suggest a continuity of development, and second to recognise that the peoples of the Empire had thrown in their lot with the mother country in the struggle against fascism. The book emphasised the drawing together of forces. The first 13 pages are therefore concerned with showing the war efforts of each of the dominions and colonial areas. The fact that there had been considerable unwillingness to participate inside both India and South Africa remains, of course, unmentioned. A brief background history of each of the areas is also given. Then the book moves to deal with its sub-title promise 'The countries of the Empire, how they are governed, and the life and work of their peoples'. As the main title suggests, the book is 80% or more illustrations, with little text. The captions, therefore, become particularly succinct and condensed. In format and style the book has much in common with the armed forces titles with which it was a near contemporary, and which are discussed elsewhere.

An undercurrent of awareness of imminent change runs through this title however. There was a tacit realisation that the ethos of empire had already passed. Although the title on the spine and title page includes the word Empire the end-papers carry the words 'British Commonwealth of Nations'. Echoes of these words are also scattered throughout the text.

Within a year another book dealing with the whole 'wider world' had appeared. This was a strange title, given the year in which it came out, *History of the World* (1944). It was in fact a very different book from the others we have discussed. It is for a start a very 'academic' social and political history. A conscious effort is made to establish the credentials of the editor, and the fourteen other figures who have contributed a chapter each. It has school and college implications, as well as appeal to the intellectually inclined autodidact. The 960 pages of continuous text are relieved by only the occasional map, and the subjects covered are, in order: Civilisations of the Near East; the glory of Greece; the Roman World; the Story of Persia; Mongols, Tartars and Turks; the Peoples and Religions of India; China and Japan; Islam and Christendom; the End of the Middle Ages; the Beginning of Modern Times; Reason and Revolution; Fifty years of Progress; Nationalism and Internationalism; The Latest Age, and an epilogue. The developments in the late 1930s and the years of war are accounted for briefly, but in other respects this is a standard history of its kind. The year of publication is very curious, though other publishers were also engaged in putting out esoteric titles at this time. The format is of the Odhams reference book size. The end-papers are hand drawn, showing the main periods and progression with which the book deals. Carlyle's 'mot' – What is all knowledge but recorded experience and a product of History? – acts as a frontispiece, and it may point to the fact that the book, by its very scope, helped people to make sense of the chaos of the war years, and fit them with a pattern.

Matters are reversed with our next title dealing with the wider world. The content of the book is surprising, but the date of its publication is not. We are discussing *From Empire to Commonwealth*

(1949). The book is relatively slim (240 pages) and in normal hardback format. 1949 seems a fitting year for a publication with such a title, when the Empire, as it had been before the war, was on the verge of breaking up, and was in that year already in the process of transforming itself into a union of self-governing dominions and territories – the Commonwealth. What this volume does is to trace the path to this end in an unusual but meaningful way. The subtitle is 'The Principles of British Imperial Government', and as Jack Simmonds' preface states:

This book may be called a political anthology. It is designed to illustrate some principles of modern British Imperial Government through a selection of original documents in which those principles were set forth and developed... This book is not intended for the specialist, but for the general student of history...

After a 30 page introduction which is partly a historical summary, and partly an assessment of the documents reproduced, the text that follows consists of a selection of documents for the whole of the British colonial area presented in chronological order from the late 15th century to the middle of the 20th. It represents a valuable source book for students at school and college level. The exoneration of British policy from accusations of exploitation is fairly mild, and shortcomings are admitted. It is yet another example of Odhams successfully adapting its choice of titles to the march of events. Because the original documents were written by the people concerned the net effect might be to produce in the reader a sense of pride at what Britain was said to have achieved. To a more modern reader the book has a bitter-sweet taste in view of the strife that followed in most areas where the colonial power withdrew.

Before leaving the theme of the wider world it is worth noting that 1946 saw the appearance of ***The World's Peoples and How They Live***. It represented a post-war version of ***Peoples of the World in Pictures***, but on this occasion with an updated text and a more equal balance between text and illustrations. For a great many Europeans and their colonial peoples the conflict had made the world seem smaller. Cultural differences, even between allies, were brought out more sharply, and this title put the cultures of different groups to the fore.

Odhams changing and developing view on the wider world, as reflected in the titles discussed, followed very closely that of British society at large, if we are to judge by other publishers' productions, and views expressed in illustrated magazines of the time. There is no real reason why this should not be the case.

As the 50s lapsed over into the 60s the world became perceptibly smaller for most people. This was not only the result of faster and better transport, but also the impact of moving images of the wider world, broadcast into the living room by the agency of television. The Belgian couple Armand and Michaela Denis, with their series 'On Safari' (1955+) brought Africa into every home. There were also feature films such as 'Born Free', and radio series like 'The Flying Doctor'. Moving images had a direct appeal, and books had now become only one of many 'windows on the world' (TV's 'Panorama' had begun in 1953). Nevertheless Odhams had done their bit in broadening the horizons, quite literally, of large numbers of ordinary folk

Gerda called to the wooden soldiers, thinking they were alive.

CHILDRENS' BOOKS

I grew up with Odhams childrens' books, and they hold a special place in my affection. In many cases I read them straight from the print. I went on reading and re-reading them well into my teens – and images and sayings from them have stayed in my memory. These titles for children started to appear in the early 1930s, and went on almost to the bitter end of Odhams existence, when some of their titles were already bearing the Hamlyns imprint.

The initial books concerned nearly all had the words 'gift', 'wonder' or 'treasure' in their titles, often with addition of the word 'golden' e.g. *The Golden Wonder Book for Children*. They were in large album size format with adequate size font for 'guided reading', or reading by the child receiving them. They were lavishly illustrated, in colour, the images drawn by illustrators of repute. They could be enjoyed by the very young for the illustrations alone. In addition to the colour plates, by the late 1940s and 1950s there were also wonderful woodcuts at the head and foot of some pages. Endpapers were often coloured and filled with engravings reflecting the books' contents.

The social and individual morality they portrayed was 'progressive' yet also remarkably staid, almost Victorian. There was a general assumption of childhood innocence. It was well into the comic era of *The Eagle* and its sister comics before this was seriously challenged. By and large the contents were already published childrens' stories by classical authors, some traditional tales and fables, and in most a smaller selection of contemporary stories. Looking at the acknowledgements it does not seem as though many writers were actually commissioned to provide material.

The term 'annual' which was sometimes used to describe these volumes was not strictly accurate. They were in essence presents to be given on birthdays or holidays such as Christmas. An advertisement in the *Daily Herald* from December 1942 promised *The Favourite Wonder Book* in time for Christmas, and at a preferential price. These books were compendia, but not derived from a magazine or other regular publication. The average length of each story was dictated by the perceived age of the child reading or being read to. The scope of each tale was enough for bedtime or rainy afternoon reading. In addition to prose and entertaining images the childrens' titles also contained short poems – some classics, others well known verse by contemporary poets such as Masefield which were destined to become classics in their turn. It was simple verse, usually strongly rhymed and fairly easy to memorise.

A list of the contributors to the 1938 *Favourite Wonder Book* makes interesting reading. The authors included: P.G. Wodehouse, A.A.Milne, Eleanor Farjeon, L.A.G. Strong, Karel Capek, Maurice Baring, A.P.Herbert, E.E.Nesbit, Geoffrey Dearmer, Lord Dunsany, O'Henry and Ronald Frankau, not all of them immediately recognised as primarily childrens' writers. The child beginning to read them would already be on the second or third rung of the ladder to reading 'adult' fiction by the same writers.

This volume was distinctly more 'modern' than the *Children's Wonder Book* of 1933, and the *Golden Wonder Book* of 1934. In the earlier of the two children's 'classics' dominated, e.g. Robinson Crusoe, Robin Hood, Sindbad the Sailor, and A Christmas Carol. Well known children's authors from the early decades of the twentieth century came to the fore in later versions of these children's books.

While contributors to the story and poem content varied the illustrators seem in many cases to have been active in the production of more than one book. Their illustrations, often deliberately quirky, have surely stayed alive in the imaginations of two or three generations of children. They were a fairy tale escape world during the emotional and economic stress and hardship of the war and the years immediately following. Now, in the twenty-first century, they are still a fond living memory for many over sixties.

To accompany these compendia of prose and poetry Odhams also produced reference books which were a junior version of those for adult readers. In the event although many of these included the word 'children's' in their title they were in no way talking down to their young readers or using patronising language. What made them more acceptable to younger readers was the editing out of the obscure, remote, complex or obtuse factography of some of the 'grown-up' texts – it was a little bit like grown men wearing full length trousers and boys also wearing trousers, but only as far as the knees. The use of the word 'wonder' or 'wonderful' in the title also suggested books that would be accessible to younger readers because of their assumed eagerness to learn new things, and possibly less attractive to adult readers.

Alongside *The Childrens' Golden Treasure Book* (1946) which contained the usual mix of classic and modern contributors, but also 'games, riddles and puzzles', there were to follow: *The Childrens' Own Book of the World* (1948), *The Practical Encyclopedia for Children* (1949), *The Childrens' Illustrated Encyclopedia of Knowledge* (1956), *The Odhams Encyclopedia*

for Children (1959) and *Every Child's Answer Book* (1961). In addition there were texts with titles such as *The Wonderful Story of the Sea* (1950) and T*he World's Greatest Wonders* (1952). These latter were, one suspects, read by adults and children, although ostensibly bought for the latter – 'so that they could learn something'.

Amongst the portfolio of Odhams' illustrated periodicals was a significant number of children's comics - the best known of which were *Eagle*, *Girl* and *Mickey Mouse.* For the last mentioned, for younger children, story-lines were written by even such outstanding figures as Enid Blyton. Other equally well-known writers were involved in contributions to all three, and to other comics. These publications were far from being pulp fiction.

Many of the comics, including the three mentioned, spawned annuals, and this is where the comics overlap with the books we have been discussing. This is particularly true of the late 'fifties, 'sixties, and even the early 'seventies. There were also stand-alone collections of comic strips, such as, inevitably *The Wonder Book of Comics* and the *Golden Book of Comics*. These book collections curiously blended comic strip and 'normal' prose narrative. *The Ace Book of Comics*, for example, bears the sub-title 'Fun and Fiction for Boys and Girls', as though comic strips alone would somehow have been insufficient.

Another of Odhams' magazines was *Picturegoer*, and this also had an associated book in the form of *Picturegoer Annual*, though this was for an adult audience who wanted 'pin-up' photographic images of 'starlets', many of whom left little trace after a few years, there was also a child reader-ship, created by the success of Saturday morning pictures, at their height in the 1940s and 1950s.

There is one other category of titles which can safely be classified as reading for children. These were small format pocket books on planes, trains, flowers, dogs, etc. They appeared under the imprint Hippo Books and, although aimed obviously at children, will be discussed in a later chapter. They appeared from 1962 -3. In 1967, by arrangement with the Sunfresh soft drinks firm even smaller booklets of a similar kind were available in return for purchasing Sunfresh drinks. The booklets were described on the cover as Odhams colour books and will also be referred to again later.

For this category of books it became practice to use the imprint Longacre Books, after the address of the firm's London office. As we have seen in an earlier section, they were a mild attempt on the firm's part to cash in on the success of the Observer and I-spy series.

Throughout the period we are dealing with Odhams had also been active in producing books for the slightly older secondary school child. The hefty 12-volume *Wonder Book of Knowledge* appeared probably, since it is undated, in the late '30s to judge by its style and binding. It was profusely illustrated and the end-papers contained a melange of the logos referred to in a previous chapter. The format, at 10 ½ x 7 1/2 inches, was considerably larger than any of the other Odhams encyclopedias, and related more to the atlases and art books they produced. *The Young People's Encyclopedia* (1958) returned to the smaller format, had end-papers of a modernistic multi-coloured design, and was also heavily illustrated.

Odhams Encyclopedia for Children (1959) saw a return to the larger format. It claimed to be, and was, 'profusely illustrated in full colour'. From the illustrations it seems safe to say that the book was intended for use by 10-year-olds upwards. Great care had been taken to give credibility and

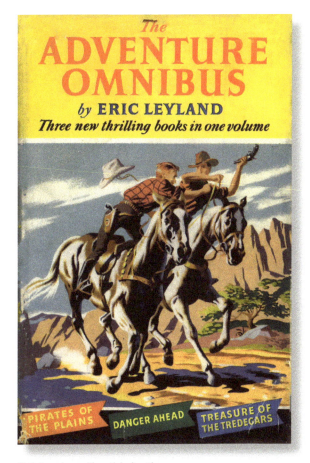

Publications like this both came out of and fed in to 'Saturday Morning Pictures' at one's local cinema.

status by listing as 'advisory editors' a London University Professor of Comparative Education, J.A.Lauwerys, a former head of Harrow School, R.W.Moore, and, inevitably, Brian Vesey-Fitzgerald, described here as 'naturalist' writer and broadcaster. He was of course a regular contributor to Odhams books that had anything to do with nature.

The last in this category was **The New Modern Encyclopedia Illustrated**. Note the almost desperate claim to topicality made by the title! It came out in 1961, and went on being reprinted until 1968, making it one of the last of Odhams factual reference books. Comparing the four titles one is very much aware of the improvements in printing technology over the years 1935 to 1968.

As the 1960s turned into the 1970s it became obvious that the books Odhams could go on producing, later in cooperation with Hamlyns, but initially without, were children's titles. Some now were admittedly derivative, based on TV series such as Magic Roundabout, but others were straightforwardly titles for the younger child reader. One series was marketed as the Odhams Magic Roundabout Mini-books, and were akin in content and format to the board books for the younger child put out by many other publishers. The firm was also involved in producing Early Learning type titles, which was very much a 1970s subject.

It is now not difficult to see why some of Odhams last productions should have been of this kind. Children's reading matter was a largely unchanged market, and whereas the appeal of the Wonder books may have diminished there was still a good take-up for the kind of books described above. Practical Man and Practical Woman may have disappeared and other media sources of information may have ousted the encyclopaedic volumes, but the early learning needs of children still remained.

In general Odhams' output of childrens' titles should be seen against the background of developments in another most important branch of the media – radio. Whereas at the beginning of the 1920's ownership of wireless sets was largely restricted to better off families, by the end of the war virtually every household in Britain had access to a radio. One of the most significant events on radio as far as this survey is concerned was the establishment in 1922 of a programme especially for children – Childrens Hour. Under the direction of Derek McCulloch the programme was at its peak in the years 1933 to 1950 and its content mirrored and in turn fostered children's books of the period. Its values were unashamedly Reithian and it overlapped with titles like the Wonder books in gently introducing its young listeners to the classics and to 'quality' serials. It is hardly possible to imagine the gentle world of the Wonder books without the comfortable sounds of Childrens' Hour.

If we put this together with the relationship of Odhams to TV discussed above, we can see that the firm's output formed part of a total cultural package through the filter of which at least three generations of the British population received their social and moral values.

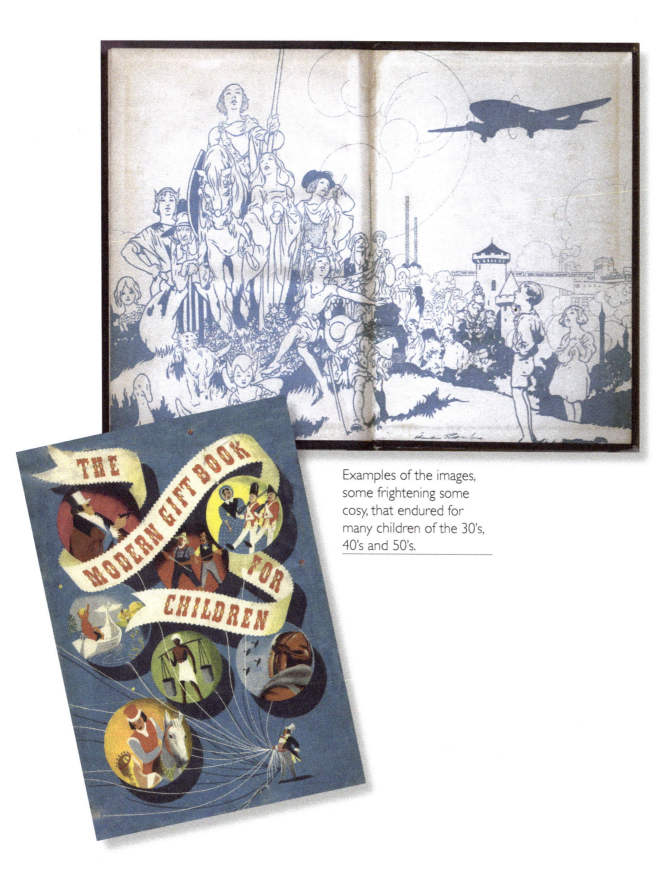

Examples of the images,
some frightening some
cosy, that endured for
many children of the 30's,
40's and 50's.

Reassuringly calm explanations of military process and tactics are presented in the pages of **Britain's Modern Army**. The powerful illustration of the endpaper for **Warfare Today** gives a stronger hint of the dramatic nature of the period

A BRITISH 3.7-INCH. A.A. GUN

These powerful guns have proved very successful. They are mobile and have an all-round traverse. The man in the right foreground is sighting the gun while the others load it

108

CHAPTER 5

The Royal Artillery

Anti-aircraft gunnery. Range-finders and predictors. Searchlights. Types of guns. A.A. organization. Coast artillery. Artillery of the field army. Anti-tank and mountain guns. Heavy guns, guns and howitzers. Divisional artillery organization. Parts of guns. Laying guns. Elementary ballistics. Observation posts and signalling. Types of gunfire

Guns, and still more guns, of every kind are wanted today, as never before. The Battle of France showed the irresistible power of boldly handled modern tanks, against a force poorly equipped with aircraft, tanks, and anti-aircraft and anti-tank guns. In the Battle for Britain, on the other hand, the fighter pilots, making up by their quality for their smaller number, won by a narrow margin. Their heroic efforts were ably seconded by anti-[...] shortage of anti-aircraft [...] several other occasions, [...] handicap to forces on th[...] When in 1914 the ant[...] made his battlefield de[...] fashion to poke fun at hi[...] inability to get his burst[...] some mile of sky as his [...] improved, and a year la[...] steady, if small, toll. T[...] combatants for the who[...] 1914-18 was one aeropla[...] rounds for every six to [...] shells fired. Striking evid[...] improvement since then [...] tion, instruments, and [...] used in the mounting [...] guns. We know that the[...] opponents have a bag of sev[...] their credit. This is a rem[...] [...]ent when one takes in[...] the vastly increased speed

improvement in performance of modern aircraft. It is heartening to know that modern guns are proving to be a more formidable menace to contemporary aircraft than were those of the last war to the much slower ones of their day.

This question of speed and the great height at which he finds his target are the two things that mark off the anti-aircraft gunner's problem from that of the field and coast artilleryman.

INFANTRY PLATOONS ATTACK ENEMY PLATOONS X AND Y

No. 1 platoon is held up by cross-fire from Y. The Bren guns of platoons 2 and 3 fire (from B) into enemy platoon X, while the mortars of Nos. 1 and 3 platoons (from A) drop a smoke-

THE SECOND WORLD WAR

Because Odhams did not actually come to the fore as a book publisher until the mid 1930s they were late in the field in terms of retrospectively reviewing the Great War, as it had come to be called. One of their only gestures in that direction was *Fifty Amazing Stories of the Great War* (1936). Even then this was part of the 'fifty' series, discussed elsewhere, rather than a separately conceived account of the war, such as other publishing houses had been producing, mostly illustrated and in large format.

But if the Great War is little reflected in Odhams output, the second global conflict is well represented. Some 20 titles appeared, interestingly enough many of them during the war itself. Despite widespread restrictions as the war progressed, both in paper, staff and other commodities vital to printing, and the removal of the book department to Kings Langley, out of range of the possibility of bombing, these titles appeared steadily from the outbreak of hostilities in 1939 to the final victory in 1946. They were sanctioned, presumably, because they could in all cases be seen as part of the war effort. Strangely enough, what might be called 'normal' output from Odhams did not cease with the outbreak of hostilities. Fifteen or so titles on subjects only loosely related to 'war effort' came out between 1939 – 45. They ranged in coverage from *The Childrens' Guide to Knowledge* (1940) to *Other People's Jobs* and *Inside Information*, both appearing in 1944. These two are interesting in that their purpose seemed to be to promote social cohesion at a time in the war when an exhausted and hungry Britain most needed it. Knowledge of how workers in various branches of industry and communications spent their working day presumably made the reader appreciate more their part in the communal effort. One knows nothing, unfortunately, of what was in the minds of the people who decided upon such titles at this particular time. It could even be that, as discussed elsewhere, their policy decisions were 'guided' by the Ministry of Information. This was particularly likely as Walter Surrey Dane, Odhams M.D., occupied a senior position in this ministry. Equally, the appearance of other more 'general', encyclopaedic titles at this particular juncture encouraged buyers to think that despite the wartime course of events there was still a degree of pre-war normality to be had.

Not surprisingly the first group of titles which had to do directly with the war effort concerned the three services. The first to appear, in 1940, was *Britain's Wonderful Fighting Forces*. With its lavish, and presumably well censored, illustrations this was, one assumes, an attempt to reassure the reader of our state of readiness. In the event its appearance coincided almost uncannily with the tragedy of Dunkirk! *Britain's Glorious Navy* appeared as the war was nearing its end, and consisted of a relating, as one might expect, of successful engagements. The preface contained an acknowledgement of the book having passed through the hands of the naval censor. Nevertheless, it did list losses. It compares curiously with *The Royal Navy Today* which had preceded it in 1942. The earlier title was much concerned, with its emphasis on 'today', with the modern nature of the navy's equipment, and by implication its superiority. It appeared in the same year as *Britain's Modern Army Illustrated*, the contents of which have a similar tone, in which respect the use of the word 'modern' in the title is of itself significant. It may very well be a reaction to suspicions that, by comparison with the Wehrmacht, the army had been somewhat less than modern at the commencement of hostilities in 1939-40, and had since then been making strenuous efforts to catch up in terms of armour and firepower. The service to which in some senses the greatest debt was owed, the RAF, achieved recognition in 1942 with the appearance of **Britain's Wonderful Airforce**. Both this title and the army book were carefully filtered, in terms of copy as well as photographic illustration, to ensure that only the official view was purveyed, and that nothing was given away when the books were read by German Intelligence and its agents, as they doubtless were.

After a two year gap, in the later stages of the war, what had become virtually another branch of the services was recognised at last with the appearance of **Britain's Merchant Navy** (1944). This title was aimed quite obviously at increasing public awareness, not only of the vital nature of the Atlantic convoys, but also an appreciation of their vulnerability. The term 'lifeline' occurs and recurs throughout the text. For all that it had propaganda value the book was also informative, and a reader knowing little about the construction and operation of merchant vessels could learn a lot from it.

Quaintly, one of the contributors speculated on what would happen to international shipping in the post-war world. Would the same busy routes apply, or would increasing amounts of freight be taken by air? In the event anyone aware of the phenomenal growth of container shipping at the ports in the UK that deal with the huge vessels involved knows exactly the answer to such speculations.

The motivation behind the appearance of all four titles is best explained by the introduction to

Britain's Modern Army, where the editor writes:

Only the highest standards of military efficiency and discipline will bring victory. In modern warfare co-operation is invaluable. Just as the three fighting services are learning to work together, and to appreciate each other, so the public too should strive to understand their work. In this way, instead of remaining uninformed critics and onlookers, we shall all become more intelligent and actively useful cogs in the total war machine.

Once the fighting forces themselves had been promoted, Odhams moved on in January 1944 to **Warfare Today**. Using material already largely covered in the books about the services this title was a full-blown examination of how the game of war was played in the 1940s. It concerns itself with tactics and strategy, with military planning, drawing on experience in the current conflict to provide examples, as well as harking back to classic battles such as the Roman wars of the fourth and third century BC. Text dominated over illustration, and the purpose of the book became clear in the opening pages:

Never before in the history of man has war been so vast a melting pot. Everything is being thrown in to be boiled down into something new. Are sea and land power to be mastered by air power? Can air power alone win a war? Can it enforce peace after the war? Or is it but one more invention which in its turn will be mastered by yet another? These and similar questions are on every lip. What are the answers? No man can say. As yet each is in itself a vast, complex problem, the solution of which will demand many answers. Nevertheless, faced as we are by this tangle of possibilities, there is a sure and certain method of procedure. It is not, like Alexander, to cut the Gordian knot, but instead to discover one of the loose ends of the tangle. This is called "Simplicity of Thought". Let us, then, seek out the simple before we plunge into the complex.

Total war was conducted in a confusing and often chaotic theatre, where it was possible for the ordinary observer to lose sight of the players, or to mis-interpret their actions. The three respected senior figures from the services who contributed to this book hoped it would go some way to resolving this problem.

Next Odhams attention was turned to what had come to be referred to graphically as the Home Front. Thus, early in 1943, there appeared *The British People at War*. It has to be said that it seems to present a very idealized picture. The images dominate the text and tend to have a symbolic, almost poster-like quality. In retrospect the tone of the introductory pages is light hearted in a somewhat inappropriate way:

> *The subsequent adventures of the average and representative citizen may be followed in these pages. The boys are in the Army, Navy or Air Force. The girls are on the land, in the munition factories, in one of the uniformed, auxiliary services. The elders are Air Raid Wardens or Home Guards. They are defenders of the Home Front….*

There was what must have been an uneasy realization that this book, with its quirky admonition that there was no longer any time for games of tennis or bridge parties, was, perhaps not taking quite the right tone. For just over a year later, in summer 1944, there appeared *Ourselves in Wartime*. Both the title and the tenor of the book were markedly different. This title was coming in at what was perceived as the level of the 'ordinary citizen', with his or her worries, stress and suffering - in so far, that is, as war censorship allowed these factors to be discussed. The heroic resilience in the face of sustained suffering under siege was indeed still pointed up, but the package containing this message was somehow subtly different from the earlier exploration of the civilian experience of the war. Text and illustration were more carefully

balanced, and the thread of continuity and normality was more strongly emphasised. A sense of reassurance was what the book aimed to give:

> *Life on the Home Front in modern war was life lived under conditions new in our land. Every phase of it felt the direct influence of the total conflict. In days of constant threat and almost continuous assault goods were manufactured, books were written, printed and distributed, crops were grown, plans for trading and supply were developed and executed, industrial, religious and social affairs were carried on, mass transfers of population were made, and the business of government administered, not at some remote base from which the fighters had been sent, but on the battlefield itself.*

The point was made that the appearance of Odhams books was itself part of the war effort – an attempt to make some normality out of what was often chaotic.

Ourselves in Wartime is also interesting because of the amount of time it spends discussing the role of women in wartime Britain. This role was increasingly being seen as vital in munitions, on the land, and in transport and support, as well as in the uniformed auxiliary services. The book gave this factor prominent recognition. In general terms this volume came nearer to the 'real people'. Of that there can be no doubt.

Interspersed between the books on the services was a tribute Odhams paid to an island that for many British people had come to symbolise heroic civil resistance to aggression. *The Epic of Malta* (1943) was obviously intended as a morale booster, both for the people of the island itself, and for Allied countries watching on. The perception of the island as a personified hero had been confirmed and reinforced by the award to Malta of the George Cross, the highest individual award made to civilians. The introduction was by

Winston Churchill.

In common with some other publishing houses, e.g. Hutchinsons, Odhams produced a multi-volume 'history' of the war. One volume was devoted to each year of the conflict, and by the end of hostilities six volumes had appeared under the title ***The First (Second, Third, etc)Year of War in Pictures***. And that is exactly what it was, a chronicle of the strategic, military and political course of the war, with many pictures, from a variety of sources, and rather smaller amounts of text to explain events and to introduce the various theatres of war. In essence it was very similar to sister publications of this kind, aimed at a market of those who wanted a largely pictorial record of what they were going through or had just been through. Sadly, Britain has been through a number of conflicts since then, and each has spawned books of this kind. It is difficult to imagine this kind of Odhams book being given as a present, but it doubtless often was.

It was probably more appreciated as a present than an earlier Odhams attempt at a 'history'. This had appeared in May, 1941. The title was curious ***The People's History of the Second World War, September,1939 – December 1940***. It consisted of over 500 pages of fairly dense copy, with the addition of numerous maps, most of which had little to do with the then incipient conflict and more to do with the politics of international relations in the first four decades of the twentieth century. The author was Harold Wheeler, a regular contributor to Odhams books which had a historical angle.

Unlike the illustrated, year by year, blow by blow account reviewed above this book seemed designed to give the layman some understanding of the causes of the war, and of the long-term issues that lay behind them. There is a strong didactic

element to the book, and it stands somewhat apart from the other 'war books', so that it is difficult to see at exactly what readership it was aimed. The use of the word 'people's' in the title suggests as wide a range of audience as possible – yet it is at times tough going, and reasonably academic.

The longed for end to the conflict, at least in Europe, eventually arrived in early 1945, and as early as July of that year Odhams marked the occasion with the appearance of ***The Victory Book*** dedicated

…to all the peoples of the world who kept the flame of freedom burning in mankind's darkest hour…

The date of appearance allowed the book to live up to its title, and to cover the later, victorious stages of the war, rather than dwelling on the dark days of the blitz and Dunkirk. It was also, naturally, much franker in its discussion of contentious issues, such as blanket bombing of civilian targets in Germany, the failure of Arnhem, and similar episodes. The scope of coverage was also wider, taking in the American role after that country's entry into the war, and the conflict in the Pacific and in Burma. It also gave great prominence to the part played by the Soviet Union, and the suffering of that country's civilian population. As a retrospective account it was considerably more comprehensive, with lavish and graphic illustrations drawn from international sources.

In 1945 blame for suffering could understandably only be laid at the door of Nazi Germany, and chapter titles such as 'German frightfulness' are both linguistically quaint and entirely typical of their time. Those over 40 who were most likely to have been involved in preparing the copy for the book, still lived the language of the 1920s and 1930s.

There is also a certain innocence about ***The***

Victory Book. It is a document from the very last stages of a world which did not yet know the Cold War or the Atom Bomb. Within months of the book's appearance the true nature of the peace, and at what cost and by what means it had been secured was to be cruelly inked in and underlined. This pseudo peace, with its ever-present threat of mass destruction, was to last a generation or more, almost until a half century had elapsed – in that new world it would never again be possible to use some of the language of *The Victory Book*.

One other text should be looked at as a footnote to the productions inspired by the war. In common with the popular press and some other publishers Odhams had in the decade before the war produced a number of books about the royal family, a subject which is dealt with in its own right in another chapter. As an answer to a question that might have been in the minds of some of 'the British People at War' there appeared in 1945 *The Royal Family in Wartime*.

This title was in the larger format which Odhams used then and later for books about royal events and personages. This book was, in fact, 'prepared', and the copy presumably provided by the council of the King George's Jubilee Trust, and the chairman of Odhams (a member of the trust) gifted all the proceeds of the sale to this charity. As with other 'royal' titles it was lavishly illustrated with high quality photographs. Well over sixty per cent of the book was illustrations in this record of the royal family's engagements during the war. Looking back from November, 1945, when the book came out, it was now possible to record many of the occasions when the King and Queen were themselves in physical danger during the course of their 'service to people and empire'.

Books to do with war issues did not stop, of course, with the coming of peace. The wounds caused by blitzkrieg, civilian suffering, military retreats and loss of life, would naturally take many years to heal. Yet now the reader had a chance to stand back from the actual conflict and examine at leisure some of the personalities amongst victors and vanquished. This process began in 1945 with the appearance of *The Life and Times of Winston Churchill*. Then the villains were subjected to scrutiny with *Goering* (1951) and Alan Bullock's seminal work *Hitler: A Study in Tyranny* (1952), although it was some twelve years, in 1964, before a study of Mussolini appeared from Odhams.

Some of the military action of the war was recalled in *Epic Stories of the Second World War* (1957), one of the few Odhams books to be printed outside Britain (in Deventer, Netherlands). After that the attention of both reading (and now viewing) public and publishers moved on.

Endpaper from **The Coronation Book of Queen Elizabeth II**
Sumptuous imagery for the Coronation of the present Queen.

THE ROYAL FAMILY

Odhams book production had developed to almost full momentum in virtually the same year as the country celebrated the silver jubilee of George V. It is not surprising therefore, that the occasion was marked by the appearance of **The Silver Jubilee Book** (1935).

One important point has to be made at this juncture. Decent reproductions of original photographs were a new feature of '20s and '30s publishing. The market for illustrated books grew rapidly, and kept step with the visual images created by cinema and the fledgling television. Publishers were therefore on the look out as it were, for subjects to illustrate. We are in fact at the very beginnings of what was to become known, a little dismissively unfortunately, as the 'coffee table' book, a book of interest, topical, but to be seen, thumbed through, rather than actually read with concentrated attention. Thus, using a royal celebration as a starting point enabled Odhams to gather together in one volume representative photographic images from the previous 25 years – all that was needed was a loose structure, a minimal amount of copy to introduce the period year by year. The royal family provided the time-span and the occasional ceremonial event – the rest was the illustrated history of 25 years. In this respect this title was closely related to the other illustrated 'histories' discussed elsewhere. As we have seen, it was part of the response to the cinema (Pathe) newsreel era. And this kind of book was not unique to Odhams.

Events surrounding the royal family following the jubilee gave Odhams the stimulus for the production of further celebratory titles. The first of these was **The Coronation Book of George VI and Queen Elizabeth** (1937). This set the style, if not quite the format, of subsequent titles of this kind. After a brief introductory section (31 pages) to the background and the ceremonial itself the rest of the 500-odd pages was made up of pictures, mostly of the press agency and newspaper kind, with a few studio-type portraits of the main participants. This was not surprising given Odhams publishing portfolio. It was the same technique as employed in the illustrated magazines.

The abdication of Edward VIII was covered very briefly, and almost entirely from the angle of the stress and anxiety it may have caused the future George VI. It was a book of a presentation kind, sumptuous in appearance, and as such it must have had a large market not only in the home country, but throughout the Empire as it then still was. Dog-eared used copies are rare. The book has normally stayed well-preserved, albeit, one suspects, as a result of being little looked at in the last sixty years.

Sadly, George VI ruled for only a few years, though they were turbulent years as far as his subjects were concerned, encompassing war, privation, threatened invasion, the onset of the collapse of empire, and the barely perceptible yet distinct beginnings of deep, fundamental social changes which would transform Britain and the status of the monarchy in the 1950s and 1960s.

Odhams produced a further number of 'royal' books in the years concerned, some prompted by the change of monarch in 1952, but others simply reflecting a changed and changing public attitude. The ordinary man and woman now wanted to know more about the everyday life of their rulers, and they were not interested solely in the ceremonial occasions.

The post-war titles began (1945) with **The Royal Family in Wartime,** discussed earlier under the heading of the Second World War. They then moved on to a more general, up-to-date view **The Royal Family** (1950), and, following her marriage to Philip Mountbatten, **Princess Elizabeth, Duchess of Edinburgh** (1950). The style of these publications was different from the pre-war Jubilee and Coronation books. These titles were slimmer, and of a slightly smaller format. They followed the life and background of the personages concerned, and included some ceremonial occasions, but also a fair sprinkling of studio portraits and posed domestic scenes. They represented a popularising tendency, and one which ran parallel to similar developments in other media, particularly, again the popular cinema newsreel. Although there were doubtless questions of protocol they seem on the surface easy books to make and assemble.

The two royal princesses, Elizabeth and Margaret, attracted great public attention, and readers wanted to know more about how they had spent their childhood, where they had been schooled, what they wore – it was the emergence of a 'democratic' tendency that became more and more marked as the years went by. To mark this growth of interest, in 1952 there appeared **The Little Princesses**. In fact by the time it came out neither of the princesses was exactly little any more. Further publications appeared on Elizabeth's accession to the throne in the same year. The first, and easily anticipated, was **The Coronation Book of Elizabeth II**. It is interesting to compare this with the previous coronation title of 1937. On this occasion the book is significantly smaller, and a generally much less lavish production. In common with the other 'royal' books the text to image ratio is something like 35/65%. In general it is still a presentation book, but of a less bulky and less ostentatious kind. Once the coronation was passed, it was a matter of public interest to look more closely at the new queen's husband – and therefore in 1953 Odhams produced **The Duke of Edinburgh – a Pictorial Biography**, the title giving an accurate description of this kind of book. In the same year a further pictorial biography appeared, and that was **Queen Mary- her Life and Times**. Queen Mary was the oldest member of the central nucleus of the royal family – she brought together in her person the age of Empire of George V and the New Elizabethan age of the young queen.

Seven years later, when media attention had shifted to the Queen's younger sister, there appeared **Princess Margaret – a Pictorial Record of her Life and Wedding**. Essentially it was the same kind of book as the titles that had preceded it, using archive images and contemporary press agency sources. It was to be the last of the 'royal' books. By 1960 Odhams was moving away from some of its previous activities, and television was beginning to have greater impact as a source of public information about royal 'celebrities'.

Odhams had covered events in royal circles for more than twenty years, mostly by pictorial means. Other publishers had done the same, their books both fostering and satisfying a public craving to somehow get closer to royal figures. No other single family gave rise to so many titles. Beyond the lifetime of Odhams the marriage of Prince Charles to Lady Diana Spencer gave rise to a fresh batch of such books.

There can be no doubt that the readers of Odhams illustrated magazines, particularly **Woman**, had provided a rich market for books of this kind, and would continue to do so for other publishing houses.

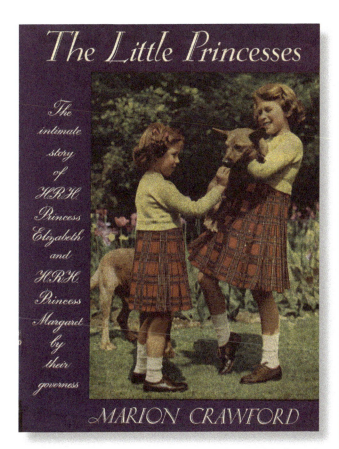

Along with formal portraiture, Odhams brought more intimate images of the Royal Family to the wider public.

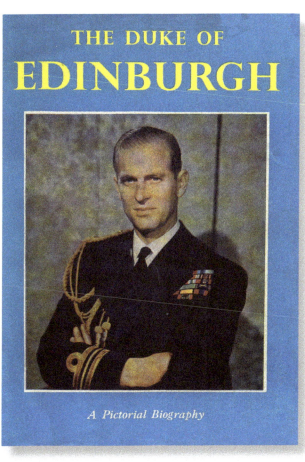

Survivors.
Photographed in 2016 in an East Anglian house, a Norfolk cottage, and a Thetford restaurant, these handsomely bound volumes were designed to encourage purchasers to make a collection of them. The perfectly-fitting bookcase shown here may well have been part of such a promotion.

SERIES' PUBLICATIONS AND COMPENDIA

Attention has already been drawn elsewhere to the fact that Odhams undertook the publication of several series of uniformly bound and formatted books with the aim of encouraging purchasers to make a collection of them. The first occasion on which this occurred, as we have seen, was the collection of Dickens and other classic authors in the 1930s.

Between 1934 and 1939 there also came out the 'Big Book of....' or even 'Mammoth Book of...' series. These were uniformly bound and presented, and were nearly all of about the same length. *The Big Book of Needlecraft* and *The Big Book of Gardening* have already been quoted. These were part compendia and part formed the basis of a potential 'library' which purchasers could assemble. They were also reference books par excellence.

If we turn to fiction, then a fascinating 'series' appeared in the same decade, and in the course of the time span roughly 1934-9. This was the 'Fifty' series, each volume containing fifty short stories from the same subject area. These subject areas were extremely varied, and some are listed below —

Amazing Stories of the First World War

Murders, Ghosts and Mysteries

Great Short Stories

Most Amazing Crimes of the Last 50 Years

Disasters and Tragedies

Great Sea Stories

Strangest Stories ever Told

World Famous Heroic Deeds

Events that Amazed the World

Great Mutinies, Rebellions etc.

Adventures into the Unknown

Greatest Stories of Love and Romance

These titles were all roughly 760 pages in length, cumbersome to handle, and not the sort of thing to be slipped into the bag or pocket for perusal on the journey to work, for example. They were more likely to be read in the comfort of the home, before the sitting-room fire, or on retiring to bed. Although the contents could only be described as light reading, the books themselves were anything but light.

If the titles suggest a degree of sensationalism then this is probably an accurate interpretation. The works concerned were in many cases by well-known authors, but the 'shock, horror' surrounding the stories is more commensurate with popular journalism, than with even middle-brow fiction. Sensation-seeking, variety-seeking, and short attention span — all suggest a particular kind of readership. It is tempting to relate this to the short stories carried at the time by, for example, the London evening papers, and to the readership of the now defunct **News of the World**, or of Odhams own Sunday paper **The People**. Copies of the Fifty series are today very well-preserved, often, one suspects, as a result of being read only once or twice, and then put aside, rather than being constantly referred to. Their effect was soon surpassed by the only too real horrors of the Second Wold War, and by the intrusion of other media, radio and television, the now well established cinema, and of course the tabloid press, all of which 'did' sensationalism much better and more immediately than a volume which demanded quite a high degree of literacy and concentration.

On a similar level was the 'Condensed' kind of book, best represented by **World Famous Books in Outline** (1939). It was a title that proved popular enough to be reprinted in 1946 and 1948. It was, by modern standards, a fairly hefty volume, but not much more so than contemporary hardback fiction. The book was subdivided by genre with fifteen-page or so excerpts from 22 of the world's major novels, followed by ten-page or so summaries of five epics, including **Faust**, **The Aeneid** and **The Nibelungen**. These are then followed by excerpts from Bunyan, Ibsen and Swift, and the book ends with similar excerpts from works of religion and philosophy, including Darwin, Marx and Thomas More. Always the excerpts brought out salient points in the plot and mood of the book in question.

The aim of such a book is presumably to give a taster of each of the novels/epics involved and to draw the reader on to closer acquaintance with the 'classics'. As the introduction to a fifty(!) page excerpt from **War and Peace** rather ingenuously puts it –

> *'To be appreciated fully the book*
> *must be read in its entirety...'*

- ingenuous because as a remark it is applicable in equal measure to all the excerpts – but obviously grotesquely so with reference to Tolstoy.

Who would buy and read such a book, and in sufficient numbers to warrant two re-printings? Students? Autodidacts? Libraries? – or possibly, and cynically, culture snobs who wanted to impress others with their knowledge of the classics. Whatever the market, the book remains a 500-odd page treasure trove of famous episodes from literary masterpieces, and key passages from great works of philosophy and religion.

Distilling multiform information and entertainment into a single volume seems to have been a fashion for Odhams in the late 1930s, and to a certain extent this lapped over into the late 1940s, interrupted by the paper shortages of the war years. Quite who it was who was going to carry around these weighty tomes is not certain – but carried around they doubtless were, like the **Mystery Book** (1934) for example, which was there for anyone wanting a daily dose of this kind of tale.

One of the initial titles of this kind, which gave rise to several decades of imitators was **The Holiday Book** (1934). Here we have a book of an even greater, weightier size than the Fifty series, intended to form part of someone's holiday luggage. It contains over a thousand pages of short stories by a range of authors, some now largely forgotten, others still well known. The contents are placed into three categories; Tales of Wit and Humour; Tales of Love and Romance; Tales of High Adventure. Amongst the better known writers included are: Dickens, Chesterton, A. A. Milne, H.G.Wells, P.G.Wodehouse, Maupassant, Bret Harte, Eden Philpotts, Oscar Wilde, and many others. The fifty stories selected offer something for everyone. But what, one may well ask, was the relationship between this wide ranging anthology and holidays? A lengthy and rather rambling foreword by the two editors provides some answers, principally that, as well as the 'normal' holidays, spent inactively lying on the beach in the sun, etc –

...sometime you will want a book. For these hours this book has been made – but it claims to be more than a book of holiday reading. It is in itself a holiday that you may take at any time without stirring from your chair, a spiritual holiday which will give you the essential change of place and people, and an endless variety of new experiences and exciting living.

- lofty aims, albeit delivered with a dash of flippant tongue in cheek. The defence of the book then, if it needed one, was that it was providing a variety of reading experiences in short enough gobbets, perhaps, to be digested at one reading session. (An aim not significantly different from some of the children's books). The idea that reading might fill those idle holiday hours when it rained (or was too hot!), or simply when idleness *was* holiday, is pure 1930s and 1940s. Not yet the DVDs, computer games, or the videos or simply watching TV – instead, reading, and at a fairly high level of literacy too. Looking back from the twenty-first century it is still hard to imagine a potential market for such a weighty tome.

Yet the anthology genre obviously worked for Odhams. Two sister titles **The Mystery Book** (1934), already mentioned, and **The Great Book of Humour** (1935) appeared with much the same readership in mind. In the non-fiction field for which there was apparently also a potential readership **One Hundred Great Lives** came out in 1939.

It was ten years later before the next book of this kind appeared, and then, as one might expect, in a much altered style and format, and significantly directed almost exclusively at women readers. **Woman** was one of Odhams most successful magazine publications, at one time it was calculated that more than $8^{1}/_{2}$ million UK women read it, and it spawned a number of related book titles

– based largely on the content of the magazine such as the **Woman Cookbook**, discussed elsewhere. It also gave birth to two what might be called anthologies – **Woman Weekend Book No.1** (1949) and **Woman Weekend Book No.2** (1950).

As the foreword to the first carefully explains, these annual publications were selections from the magazine over the preceding year. Nothing was specially written, bar the foreword, for these weekend books. Number one appeared in November, 1949, and its purpose was laid out straight away –

This book is really a compromise. It includes many features and stories which received notable welcome from our readers, and it also includes recipes, articles, stories, and other features which the staff of Woman *think worth republishing in book form. This anthology of the best of* Woman *is, therefore, chosen jointly by our readers and ourselves.*

With memories of the enormous tomes of 1939 possibly in mind the editors set out to make:

...a book which would be handy to hold and convenient to slip into a weekend suitcase, or onto a bedside table.

So, like The Holiday Book there was an assumption of reading done outside the normal weekly routine. Unlike The Holiday Book, however, the weekend books were more truly portable, and certainly more comfortable to hold.

The contents remained in basically the same proportions from year to year. There were short stories allegedly popular with Woman readers, usually about ten or twelve stories, quite short, not more than ten or twelve pages long. Most, but by no means all, were about love and romance. The remaining hundred or so pages were taken up with –

...interesting and instructive hints on Beauty, Housewifery and Personal Problems, Cookery Knitting, and useful things to make.

By the twenty-first century Housewifery has already become an archaic term. From a domestic point of view these post-war magazine-related books also contained sections called 'Tackling it together' where both wife and husband are encouraged to undertake renovating or decorating together. It was a move away from the pre-war view, and had been brought about largely by wartime experience.

The reference to personal problems is also of this time. Most womens' magazines, and some daily papers, ran an 'agony aunt' column, and **Woman**, with Evelyn Home, was no exception.

Childrens' literature also reflected the fashion for compendia. Late in 1949 Odhams brought out **The Adventure Omnibus** referred to elsewhere. It was a single volume containing three newly written stories by Eric Leyland. It was regarded by the publishers as a childrens' book, and aimed at the adolescent boy. It was six years later before the appearance of **Adventure Stories for Girls** (1955). The novelettes, crime, wild west and treasure-seeking now seem stagey in retrospect, and pitched at a largely middle-class readership. Not surprisingly they have something of the atmosphere of the BBC's Childrens' Hour of the 1940s. Nevertheless they mirrored publishing for adults in the way they were presented – three for the price of one, and something for everybody.

One of the last gestures made by Odhams in the direction of this kind of book was **The Book of Leisure** (1957). It also aimed to be a weekend or bed-side book, as the publishers described it. It was unusually well-illustrated, with numerous line-drawings and coloured and black and white photographs. It was vaguely male in orientation of contents, and was the counter image of the **Woman** books, but contained much more that was half fiction, half documentary sketch. There was even the occasional piece of humorous verse. The foreword by John Pudney, a writer popular at the time, says:

> *Most of the writing here has been done specially for* The Book of Leisure. *A very few pieces have appeared before in print, or on the air in a different form... we have gone about this book in a way that befits our theme. Yet I hope we shall not put any reader to sleep who is not predisposed to slumber. We should like to consider ourselves in any case a bedside book, so that even the really busy people may come to us in the end.*

This light, frothy and almost flippant tone pervades the whole book. Writers such as H.E.Bates, Louis Golding, Compton Mackenzie, A.P. Herbert and Arthur C. Clarke were all, as critics, newspaper contributors, radio personalities, familiar to a middlebrow audience/readership, and very popular. In many ways it was simply an example of good quality light reading – and in that respect a worthy successor to **The Holiday Book** over twenty years earlier.

'SERIES' PUBLICATIONS FOR NON-FICTION

In addition to omnibus, condensed or encyclopaedic titles, Odhams also published over this period a number of uniformly bound books, with the intention that the purchaser should collect them, in the same way as the Fifty, etc series for fiction referred to earlier, as they came out over a period of time, thereby forming as it were a domestic library.

A series containing the works of Dickens and other classics was one of the first to appear, and has already been referred to elsewhere. All of this is a fashion in book-buying which has by now long disappeared, since so many alternative sources of information, knowledge and enjoyment are now available, with very little searching. To a certain extent this has destroyed the time-honoured relationship and inter-relationship between various branches of knowledge – and that is to be regretted. True knowledge may well reside in such relationships.

In the same year as the classics, 1935, Odhams began a series called the **Modern Home University.** The title suggests the selling lines of 'up to date' and 'domestic' which accompanied nearly all of Odhams informational books of the period. The subjects covered ranged from **The Science of Living Things** to **Languages** and **Book-keeping**. This series was accompanied almost contemporaneously by the **Standard University**, with the same intended market, and the same range of titles. Another parallel series of somewhat smaller uniformly bound books with no umbrella title also appeared in the immediate pre-war years. It covered a wide range of subjects from keep-fit, to counselling and the law. In appearance it was not unlike Dents' Everymans series, or the informational texts published by the English University Press. These books were relatively inexpensive, and presumably appealed to a similar market. Odd volumes in this latter series carried the magic Odhams catchword 'practical'. All three of these series came to an end with the outbreak of war. With the coming of peace, the savouring of which was marred by some atrocious winters and an extended period of shortages, disruption and austerity, it was some time before Odhams were able to undertake another series. This time, as might be expected, the format was larger and more modern, the paper and the photographic illustrations of a higher quality.

The series was given the overarching title **The New Educational Library**. The first volume to appear was **French: How to Speak and Write it** (1947). Allied troops had spent some time fighting in France and French people had taken refuge in England for the duration. Although British relations with France during the war had not been easy, the country was, after all, only 20-odd miles away, and for some a daytrip to France was to become again as easy, if not easier, than a day-trip to London. The language teaching methodology was part traditional, part embracing phonetic transcription, and other more modern practices. As with many courses of this kind it was situation based, chapter by chapter, each lesson ending with exercises. The book concludes with a chapter on France and French culture. In common with other titles in this series, the text is prefaced by an impressive list of advisory editors, including many eminent names. The next volume **German: How to Speak and Write it** appeared in 1948. The war had given an impetus, not only to the spread of English world-wide, but had produced a significant and growing home market for learning foreign languages. The choice of language this time is fairly obvious, as English speakers (with their families in many cases) now formed a significant proportion of occupying forces over almost half the territory of their vanquished foe. The pattern of presentation was basically the same as for **French**.

These two languages were followed, also in 1948, by volumes on **Physical Science**, **The Arts**, and **Geography**. In the course of 1948 and 1949 sister volumes came out on subjects ranging from **Psychology** and **Economics** to **English** and **British Social History** (two volumes). Many were reprinted over the course of the following decade, some appearing in red boards and others in two-tone dark and light blue. Not all of the photographic images used were post-war, but this was forgivable, and the books represent their subjects tolerably well. As late as 1957 fresh titles were being added. As a collection they together represent a serious chunk of information. It was an impressive series, with test questions at the end of each section or chapter to aid learning and retention. Reading these titles certainly made a difference to my own schooling. Sometimes the world changed around the volumes so rapidly that they had to be revised, witness the fact that the volume on the British Commonwealth had to be virtually re-written between 1952 and 1961!

The challenge from other media, changes in schooling methods, and , later, the impact of IT, would all make it almost certain that 'series' of this kind would not continue long into the 'sixties, although Hamlyn, Dorling Kindersley and other publishers went on producing such informational volumes, some directed as much at the adult purchaser as to the child reader.

It was, in fact, in the area of children's literature

that Odhams output of 'series for collecting' persisted. In 1962-3 they produced a series (not wholly, but principally, for children) under the imprint Hippo Books, referred to earlier. These covered a range of subjects from cars to dogs, and from birds to fighter planes. There were 24 in the series and they sold at 3/- or 3/6 each. They were truly pocket books in possibly one of the smallest formats for boards and binding, as opposed to paper back. In the market they were in direct competition with the I-spy books and other extremely popular series. They took advantage of the growing habit amongst adults and children of 'spotting' things as they travelled, often on journeys in the family car. They appeared right at the start of the motorway building programme, when more and more families were seeing more and more of Britain, its towns and countryside. Because of their format if intensively used their durability was suspect, and many have reached this century with the boards and binding in a state of collapse.

Much later in the decade, in 1967/8, Odhams began a series more obviously for adults (and older children?) under the title **Exploring** e.g. **Exploring Coins**, **Exploring the Weather, Exploring the Stamp World**, etc. They were very similar in coverage to the Shire Books which still exist in this century, but very different in presentation. They appear to be based on the assumption that adults would find something of interest in them, and at the same time they would be of educational value to children, as they saw or heard things in the world around them which they were then able to read about in more depth. Because of this the style of the text is direct and fairly unsophisticated. Unlike the Shire or I-spy books Odhams **Exploring** series came in hardback book format of roughly a hundred pages, with hand-drawn illustrations. By 1968 twenty-two such titles had appeared, but by that time also Odhams days as an independent entity were numbered, and ***Exploring Canals and Waterways***, which appeared in that year, was already produced by Hamlyns 'for Odhams Books'. Nevertheless, Tinlings, one of Odhams' long-term printing partners, were even at this stage still being used.

It would be wrong to give the impression that Odhams, after the classics, was only involved in series for non-fiction – but there certainly was a long gap between the original 1930's classics and the series of much less established fiction of Odhams last years.

In the mid 'fifties Odhams began two of their own discount bookclub outlets – the Companion Book Club, and the Popular Book Club. As with other publishers' 'clubs' the book output consisted of reprints of existing successful titles. The books were available to club members at roughly one third of the 'original' price. The clubs were advertised in the firm's magazines and papers. In the initial stages of sales members were even offered a glass-fronted bookcase to house the collection. The advertisements included a reference to the motive for buying and collecting the books. It also, interestingly enough, appealed to what it saw as a latent social intellectual snobbery and one-upmanship:

The claim by the Companion Book Club to be the biggest book club 'in the Commonwealth' is significant and underlines the fact that Odham's market included many overseas sales. In the decade following the end of the war British people had been emigrating in great numbers to the dominions, and they obviously took their reading tastes and habits with them. The concentration on this relationship between books and magazine and newspaper circulations is an echo of Odhams' original stance in the 1930's.

Readers Union, Readers Digest, and Book Clubs had all for a number of years been producing series of single volume collections of contemporary short novels - some of which were in their turn to become modern classics. Odhams joined this group with a series called Mans Books. It began to appear late in the 1950's and went on until the late 1970's, by which time some of the books were carrying the Hamlyn imprint, but were also listed as being 'made and printed by Odhams books'.

These were reprints of already published works, and included no original fiction. As the name of the series suggests they were primarily intended for a male readership and were, to use a loose term, adventure novels and stories. Such a series was lucrative in the years before the final dominance of the paperback in this field. Forty years on a surprising number of these latter collections still adorn the shelves in bungalow living rooms up and down the land as some kind of totemistic offering to literature, usually sited behind the backs of those looking at the inevitable screen, but the smartly bound books look good. Lest it should be thought that few people went to the length of collecting all the volumes in the earlier series, a visit to a local saleroom dealing with house clearances will soon dispel any doubts. A box of pristine 50 series, or a complete collection of Dickens is not an unusual sight. Sadly they often remain unsold.

This area of Odhams publications included an apparently random selection of the lives of famous men, from Toscanini to Goering. Indicative of the time, there were no women featured.

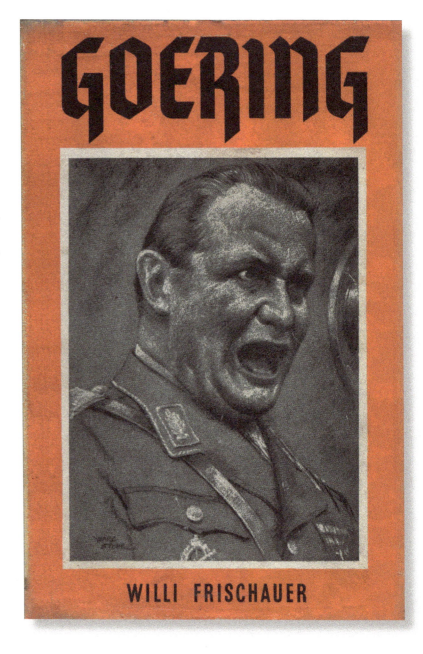

GOERING

WILLI FRISCHAUER

SINGLE VOLUME NON-FICTION AND FICTION

Many still think that Odhams published only 'reference' and 'how to' works. Yet, as we have seen, since its very inception in the first half of the nineteenth century, Odhams Ltd had been engaged, like many other publishers, in producing one-off volumes devoted to significant figures of the age.

In the period in the firm's history we are looking at three outstanding figures of the 1920's and 1930's were honoured with one-off books about them or by them. The personalities concerned were David Lloyd-George, George Bernard Shaw, and H.G.Wells. Lloyd-George's *War Memoirs* appeared in 1938, and individual works on Shaw and Wells went on appearing until their deaths.

Perhaps not surprisingly, there was a gap in this kind of title over the war years, and a subsequent flowering in the 1950's. A random selection includes the following biographical assessments – *Toscanini* (1951), *Goering* (1951), *Hitler, A Study in Tyranny* (1952). The victors found it difficult to shed their fascination with the minutiae of the lives of the foe they had just vanquished, a fascination, it could be argued, that still continues. The last mentioned book, by the historian Alan Bullock, was destined to become a classic of its time. In the years that followed there appeared volumes on *William Godwin*(1953) and *George Stephenson* (1954).

In addition there were single volumes which presented anthologies of writing by or about significant contemporary figures. Of these two can be taken at random. The first is *If I had my*

Time Again (1950), in which a number of contemporary figures from all walks of life were asked what they would do differently if they could live their lives over again. It was a quaint foray into this sort of field, but hardly at the popular level, as some of the personalities involved were, although well-respected, somewhat remote from the public gaze. Another anthology of this kind was *Victorian People* (1954). This was a collection of monographs on a selection of figures from the Victorian period deemed to be outstanding. It took for its scope the period of high Victorian ethos, between 1851 and 1867. The leading figures of this period formed the basis of the study. They included Disraeli and Dickens, to name but two. It was written by a then young and up and coming academic, Asa Briggs, who also produced a sister volume for Odhams *Victorian Cities* (1963). This second book was also rather more about public figures than about public buildings.

One of the last in this sequence, and already bearing the Hamlyn imprint, was *World Famous Exiles* (1969). It formed part of a mini series which appeared under this joint imprint, with titles such as *World Famous Trials*, *Heroes of the Twentieth Century*, etc. *Exiles* contained a very catholic range of oddly assorted figures, as one might expect, the only common factor being exile. The book included Charles II, Hemingway, Dostoevsky and Haile Selassie, as well as the more obvious Napoleon. There were in all 27 exiles, and each one was allotted some nine or ten pages of text.

Two other one-offs which represented no

particular pattern were both devoted to a place rather than a person or persons. The first of these was **The Epic of Malta,** referred to elsewhere, which came out shortly after the end of the war. The island had been the scene of fierce resistance to intensive Italian and German air strikes, and there had been heavy destruction and loss of life. The virtual personification of the island brought out by the award of the George Cross, almost lifts it into our first category. The book was moderately large in format and tended towards a pictorial history of the island's suffering.

Another 'place', as opposed to person, which proved to be of public interest because of the attention given to the role of the churches in occupied Europe, particularly, but not entirely, the Catholic Church, was the Vatican. Thus in 1950 Odhams duly produced a slim, well-bound and largely pictorial volume on the Holy City. 1950 was a Holy Year, and the aim of the book was ostensibly to celebrate that fact. The Vatican is in some ways an archaic and isolated survival from the Middle Ages, and the regimen and structure of the mini state needs quite a degree of explanation. It had occupied an anomalous position in the Italian national state created by the fascists. As a result the makeup of the book's 160 pages is roughly 50% text and 50% photographic images.

At least in the years of peace before and after the Second World War Odhams output was sprinkled with one-off fiction titles, stretching from Edgar Rice-Borroughs' **Jungle Girl** to **Recent Short Stories** (1960). Very often these texts were of good pedigree, but balanced between adult and adolescent readership. In the 1950s and 1960s many found their way onto school reading lists, often onto the reading lists of non-specialist groups in the secondary modern sector. Frequently the aim was to encourage reading generally, as a worthwhile activity. The preface to the 1960 **Short Stories** expresses it thus:

> *It is hoped that this selection of short stories will appeal to pupils of fourteen to sixteen. Except that it omits stories whose effects are too subtle or adult, it gives a representative idea of the types of short stories being written today.*

Nevertheless, the fifteen stories offered include tales by Marcel Ayme, C.S. Forester, Somerset Maugham, Dylan Thomas and H.E.Bates in his guise as Flying Officer X. The developing didactic tone of the preface makes one aware that it too was intended to be read in schools. Thus, even in this field, Odhams were intent on giving an educational value to their productions.

Occasionally, as we have seen, Odhams were reacting to a particularly topical event or personality. Probably the best example of this was the publication in 1954 of Paul Brickhill's biography of Douglas Bader, the crippled war-time air ace, **Reach for the Sky**. Bader's story captured the public imagination in a big way and two years later was made into a full-length feature film.

Among other numerous non-fiction one-offs two may be picked out at random. Once more one is from the 1950s, and the other from the following decade. The choice of subject seems at first unprompted by external factors and one might get the impression that the books come about as the result of a 'normal' publishing selection process – the work being brought to the publisher by the author, and eventual publication being decided upon by the former.

From the 1950s comes **Guardians of the Queen's Peace** (1953). It is a 250-odd page text in normal hardback format, and with a sprinkling of illustrations. The author traces the development of the British police force from earliest post-Norman Conquest times to the mid-twentieth century. It is possible to trace the origins of the book to its topicality. This arose from growing public interest in the police in the wake of the notorious Craig and Bentley case. Hitherto, both in literature and film and other media the police had been in the background, often depicted as bumbling and ineffectual by comparison with super sleuths, be they Sherlock Holmes or Lord Peter Wimsey. There were also media reasons for public interest in the day to day workings of the force, reflected by successful radio serials like PC49 (first broadcast 1947) and TV programmes such as Dixon of Dock Green (1955), and later more racy, and possibly more realistic serials such as Z Cars. The police force was something the public wanted to read about. The media had moved them into the foreground. The image put before them by this book was highly positive; once again Odhams were informing, educating and entertaining. Our own age, on the other hand has rather singled out the short-comings of the police for its attention.

From the 1960s, a decade or more away, comes *The Story of London Town* (1967). The City, the 'heart of empire', had already figured in earlier Odhams pictorial books. The capital had been thrown into the limelight, though, through most of late 1950s and early 1960s by the amount of buried history revealed in the process of reconstruction and the blitz damage itself. The book is standard hardback format and about 140 pages in length. It deals with the characters and events in London's history, as well as the architectural structures. It has no photographs, but instead hand-drawn illustrations accompany the text. The illustrations are of the kind often found in children's books of this vintage. However, despite the unsophisticated and non-academic atmosphere of the text, it would be unfair to class it solely as a children's book. It occupies instead the no-man's land between school and adult leisure reading. The half a dozen sister publications listed in the dust-jacket seem to be of the same kind, and reflect the publisher aiming at two separate, but related markets.

In general terms single title fiction and quasi fiction publication seems to be the result of Odhams responding in one of two ways, though these were often intertwined. They were either selecting an author who was a recognised classic, or one who had become or was becoming topical. This second response was also often the result of what was happening in other media, something we have already observed in the sections on gardening and cookery.

CONCLUSION

Odhams maintained a consistency of book production from the beginning of our period in the early 1930s. On average they put out 15-20 titles per year, even during wartime there was a consistent though reduced output. They had begun their books for the masses by making the classics available in practical and well-presented bindings to a wide audience. They built an extensive customer base by using the national popular press and their own portfolio of illustrated magazines and comics.

Odhams had been at the cutting edge of print technology. Their domination of photogravure processes had established them as leaders in the field of illustrated books. In this respect they were forerunners of the later coffee table books.

Also, thanks largely to the personal influence of Salter Elias, the publishing house maintained an almost 'Reithian' high moral tone virtually to the end of its independent existence in the 1960s.

There is a way in which Odhams' book output over the years of this survey can be seen as a response to a need, and the result of an acute understanding of the contemporary book market. Odhams were, admittedly, not the only publisher at this period to react to the phenomenal growth of what amounted to a new social class. Between the wars there was a rapid increase in the number of non-manual jobs – accompanied by the re-housing of a large cohort of the middle-class from inner city terraces into semi-detached suburbia. Some of the four million or more new houses involved were constructed by local authorities, but the majority were the result of speculative building initiatives. Thus, for Odhams and other publishers, there arose a potential readership consisting of a literate first time house-owning middle class that thought of itself as upwardly mobile. Towards the end of the interwar period also large numbers of light industry factories were opened in the suburbs themselves, as, for example, along the arterial roads leading out of London, so that the newly acquired family car was often a vehicle for weekend pleasure trips rather than commuting to work. The new suburban semis (the term 'villa' went on being used well on into the 'thirties) often provided a space for a garage, if not the actual structure itself. As we have seen Odhams book output managed to reflect and feed into this world.

There had been much change in the world of Odhams potential readership by the time the firm fell victim to financial difficulties, mismanaged takeovers, and changes in media and social behaviour.

In our chronological examination of some of these titles we have been aware of a society on a journey. It was a journey across three reigns; a journey from economic depression to relative prosperity; from Empire to Commonwealth; from cinema to universal television; from horses to tractors; from flying-boats to Comet jetliners; from the ostrich-like anxious insouciance of the 1930s to the relative security of the Cold War; from un-metalled roads to motorways; from self-sufficiency to wide retail choice. In the middle there had been the six years of world war – total war – bringing with it austerity, fear, shortages, civilian suffering, and ultimately a loss of national pride.

For the whole course of this journey semi-detached suburban society had remained surprisingly stable

– this was largely because it embodied the ideal we have already analysed – the ideal of 'Home', so much reflected in the titles of Odhams books. It was a home lived in by the so-called 'symmetrical' family, depicted in the illustrations of some of Odhams titles. It was a family which sought to improve itself, to develop handicrafts, gardening skills, cooking and minor building skills. It still believed in gender-based domestic roles. It had more leisure than formerly, but wanted to make this leisure creative. In this respect the introduction to ***The Universal Book of Hobbies and Handicrafts*** by Sid G Hedges expresses the philosophy at some length:

> ...*Nowadays hobbies are coming to have much greater value, for three main reasons: there is more leisure; there is the tyranny of machines; there is the economic malaise which makes it difficult for young people to choose original careers.*

> *Those of us with daily occupations have, on the whole, far more free hours than had previous generations. What is to be done with leisure?*

> *No real satisfaction comes from a mere pastime which can do no more than fritter away the hours. The value of the worthwhile hobby is that it gives benefit to mind, or hand, or muscle. It constitutes a relaxation and change from ordinary occupation. It may effect economies in expenditure, or even be a means of earning. It makes leisure a time of delight instead of dullness; of opportunity instead of oppressive boredom; of achievement instead of inactivity.*

Whatever criticism it may have attracted suburban society treated its semi as a nest, a lap or womb, from the security of which it looked out first at the Britain around it, and then the wider world. Odhams books, with their informative and illustrated texts, fed into this situation.

Overall, Odhams output helps us not only to reconstruct the past, our past, but also to explore the close relationship in this period between book publisher and the changing structure and tastes of British society.

Appendix I
A selection of Odhams books by year of publication

1923 Garden Construction etc.

1932 The Handy Crossword Companion

New Standard Encyclopaedia & World Atlas

1933 British Encyclopaedia 12 vols.

Childrens' Wonder Book

The Pageant of the Century

The Wonder Encyclopaedia for Children

1934 Britain's Wonderland of Nature

Complete Plays of Bernard Shaw

New English Dictionary

The Golden Wonder Book

The Holiday Book

The Mystery Book

The Story of the World in Pictures

The World's Greatest Stories of Love/Romance

1935 Everybody's Gardening Guide

Literary Classics (60 titles)

Practical Book-keeping, etc.

The Great Book of Humour

The Silver Jubilee Book

Universal Book of Hobbies & Handicraft

1936 Cookery & Home Management

Fifty Amazing Stories of the Great War

Fifty Most Amazing Crimes of last 50 years

Mammoth Book of Murders, Ghosts, etc.

New Illustrated Universal Reference

Story of 70 Momentous Years

The Big Book of Great Short Stories

The Universal Home Lawyer Illustrated

1937 Fifty Amazing Secret Service Stories

Fifty Great Disasters and Tragedies

Fifty Great Sea Stories

Fifty of the Strangest Stories ever told

The Cookery Book

The Coronation Book of George VI & Queen Elizabeth

1938 Big Book of Needlecraft

Everybody's Best Friend

Favourite Wonder Book

Fifty Adventures into the Unknown

Fifty Events That Amazed the World

Fifty World Famous Heroic Deeds

Fundamentals of Good English

How Much Do You Know?

Live Successfully 13 vols

Modern Cookery Illustrated

Peoples of the World in Pictures

Pictorial History of South Africa

Practical Home Doctor

Real Life Problems and their Solution

The Complete Handyman

The Golden Treasure Album of the Screen

The Miracle of Life

The Science of Living Things

The Wonderful Story of the Human Body

W. S. Churchill – My Early Life

War Memoirs of Lloyd George

Wonderful Story of London

1939 Churchill – Step by Step

Everybody's Book of Facts

Everywoman's Home Doctor

Great Contemporaries by W. S. Churchill

How It Works and How It's Done

How to Write, Think & Speak Correctly

Languages: Fr., Ger., Latin

Lovely Britain

One Hundred Great Lives

Practical Information for All

Secrets of Successful Gardening

The Book of Hints and Wrinkles

The Home Counsellor

The Home Workshop

The Modern Woman's Medical Guide

The Practical Way to Keep Fit

Universal Knowledge

1939 -40 Marvels of the Modern World

Marvels and Mysteries of Science

The Home of Mankind

1940 Britain's Wonderful Fighting Forces

Children's Guide to Knowledge

Everybody's Book of Hobbies

First Aid in the Home

Pictorial Guide to Modern Dressmaking

Romantic Britain - first edition

The Modern Standard Dictionary

1941 Countryside Companion

General Engineering Workshop Practice

Handyman Home Mechanic

The People's Hist. of Second World War

The Practical Household Guide

1942 Britain's Modern Army Illustrated

Britain's Wonderful Airforce

The Royal Navy Today

1943 Britain's Merchant Navy

Everyday Knowledge in Pictures

Modern Foundry Practice

The British People at War

The Story of the British Empire in Pictures

1944 History of the World

Inside Information

Ourselves in Wartime

The Practical Man's Book of Things to Make and Do

The Secrets of Other People's Jobs

Warfare Today

Wonders of Nature

1945 Dictionary of the English Language

Life of Churchill

Miracles of Invention & Discovery

Practical Mathematics for All

Practical Plumber & Sanitary Engineer

The Royal Family in Wartime

The Victory Book

1946 Britain's Glorious Navy

Everyday Things and their Story

The First-Sixth Year of the War 6 vols

Wild Life Illustrated

Electric Motors and Generators

Exploring Fabrics

Modern Home Nursing and First Aid

Nature Through the Year

Practical Home Mending Made Easy

Practical Printing and Binding

Railways, Ships and Aeroplanes Illustrated

Romantic Britain - second edition revised *(and shortened to half its length, leaving a tourism book, with all the chapters on myth and legend removed).*

The Children's Gift Book

The Miracle of Man

The World's Best Photos

The World's Peoples and How They Live

Triumphs of Engineering

1947 Birds, Trees and Flowers Illustrated

French (NEL)

Home Cookery Illustrated

Modern Homes Illustrated

Odhams Practical and Technical Encyclopaedia

Practical Commercial Self-Educator

Practical Family Knitting Illustrated

Practical Plastics Illustrated

The Complete Self-Educator

The World's Railways and How They Work

1948 Childrens Own Book of the World

Geography (1948) NEL

German (New Educ. Library)

Handyman's Complete Self-Instructor

Knitting Illustrated

Painting as a Past-time (with Benn)

Physical Science (NEL)

Practical Carpenter and Joiner

Practical Home Needlecraft in Pictures

Radio, Television & Electrical Repairs

The Arts (1948) NEL

The British Heritage

The Children's Gift Book

The Complete Home Entertainer

The English Counties Illustrated (1)

The Modern Gift Book for Children

The Practical Home Handyman

Worldfamous Books in Outline

1949 Economics (NEL)

From Empire to Commonwealth

How the Other Man Lives

Railways, Ships and Aeroplanes

The Ace Book of Comics

The Adventure Omnibus

The Complete Book of Motor-Cars,
Railways, Ships and Aeroplanes

The Nature Lovers Companion

The Story of the British People in Pics

Twelve Modern Short Novels

Woman Weekend Book 1

1950 Country Lover's Companion

Country Magazine

Devon & Cornwall in Pictures

English Cathedrals and Abbeys Ill.

If I had my time again

New Illustrated Gardening Encyclopaedia

Practical Gardening & Food Production in
Pictures

Practical Home Dec. and Repairs Ill.

Practical Home Handywoman

Princess Elizabeth, Duchess of Edinburgh

Rose Buckner's Book of Homemaking

The Royal Family

The Wonderful Story of the Sea

Ways of Medieval Life & Thought

Woman Weekend Book 2

1951 100 years in Pics

British Countryside in Colour

Castles and Manor Houses Ill.

English Inns Ill.

Hampshire & The New Forest in Pics

Home Counties in Pics

Home Handicrafts Ill.

Lake District in Pics

Odhams Enquire Within

Rural London in Pics

The British Countryside in Pics

The Highlands of Scotland in Pics.

The Story of the Christmas Card

1952 British Flowers in Colour

Complete Dressmaking in Pics.

Coronation Book of QEII

English Villages in Pics

Handyman's 'How To Do It' in Pics

Hitler: A Study in Tyranny

Odhams Encyclopaedia of Cookery Ill.

Shakespeare Country in Pics

The Little Princesses

Yorkshire in Pics

The Complete Book of Motor Cars,

1953 Country Wines

Guardians of the Queen's Peace

How to Choose and Enjoy Wine

Queen Mary – Her Life and Times

Questions of East and West

Road Atlas of Great Britain

Royal Homes Illustrated

The Art of Conversation

The Child's First Five Years

The Duke of Edinburgh – a pictorial biog.

The Illustrated Encyclopaedia

W. Godwin: His Life and Times

1954 Collected Shakespeare

Commonsense Cooking & Eating

Francis Wardel's Zoo Book

George Stephenson

Magnificent Journey – The Rise of the Trades Union

Modern Home Painting & Decorating

Practical Home Woodworking Ill.

Victorian People

Viscount Southwood

1955 25 Momentous Years

Adventure Stories for Girls

Gardening Without a Garden

Odhams Motor Manual (also '57)

Pressure Cookery

Pruning for Amateurs

Seventy True Stories of WWII

1956 Big Book of Gardening

Childrens' Ill. Encyclopaedia of Gen. Knowledge

Country Fayre

Historic Britain

Labour Saving Gardening

Philip Harben's Cookery Encyclopaedia

Practical Automobile Engineering Illust.

1957 Biology (NEL)

British Social History (2.vols) (NEL)

Complete Flower Gardening in Pictures

English (NEL)

Epic Stories of WWII

Historic Towns of England in Pictures

History (NEL)

Home Gardening Illustrated

Law & Government (NEL)

Mod. Childrens' World of Knowledge

North Wales in Pictures

Odhams Encyclopaedia of Needlecraft

The Book of Leisure

The World of Science & Invention

1958 Care and Cultivation of Indoor Plants

Farming: Learning & Earning

Man's Books Compilation started 1958+

Odhams Young People's Encyclopaedia

The English Counties (2nd edition)

The Ford Popular Handbook

1959 Ford Anglia and Prefect Handbook

Picturegoer Annual 1958-9

The Standard Eight and Ten

1960 Odhams Encyclopaedia of Knitting

Radio, TV and Electrical Repairs

The Scholarship Home Tutor

1961 Every Child's Answer Book (-71)

Historic Britain 1960 Rep.

Railway Operating Practice

The Book of the West

Vauxhall Victor Handbook

1962 Birds in Britain

Hippo Children's Pocket Books (onto 63)

Odhams Fashion and Dressmaking

Swift Picturebook of Buses, Coaches, Lorries

Swift Picturebook of Transport Oddities

Understanding the Countryside

1963 Longacre Book of Aircraft

Longacre Book of Cars

Longacre Book of Ships

Longacre Book of Trams

Victorian Cities

1963 Decorating with Flowers and Plants

Gardening Through the Ages

Good Driving

1964 Exploring Names

Odhams Practical Photography &

Film etc.

Triumph Herald and Vitesse Handbook

Woman Cookbook

1965 The Vauxhall Wyvern Cresta Velox Handbook

1966 Illustrated Encyclopaedia of Animal Life (collab.)

Modern Encyclopaedia for Children

1967 Exploring Pottery/Fashions & Fabrics

Practical Cookery for All

Story of London Town

Sunfresh Booklets 5 vols

1968 Exploring Canals & Waterways

1969 Fiction/Children's lit.

Individual volumes on into '70's

World Famous Exiles/with Hamlyn

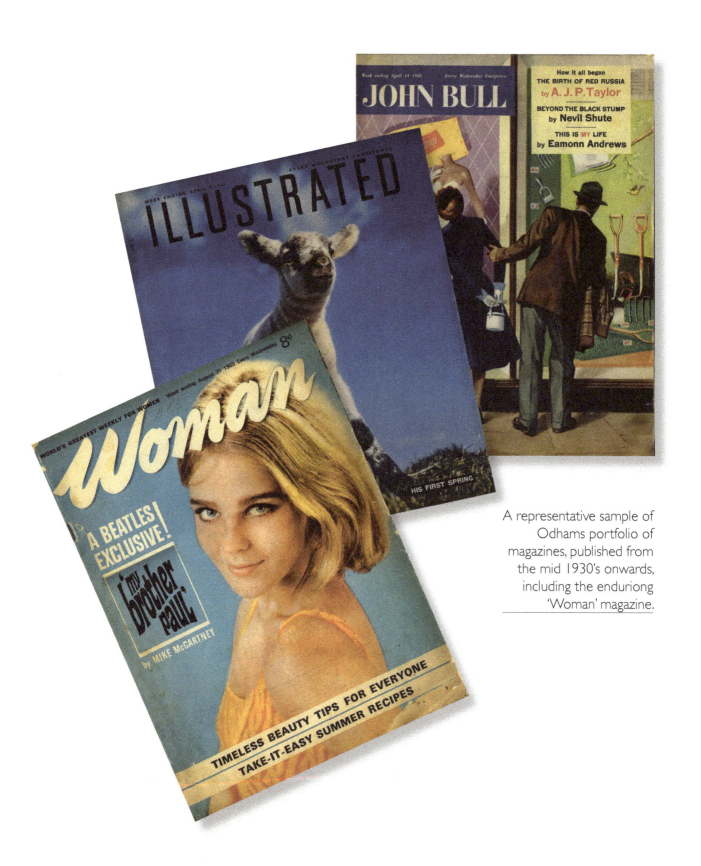

A representative sample of Odhams portfolio of magazines, published from the mid 1930's onwards, including the enduriong 'Woman' magazine.

Appendix II
Magazines and newspapers
printed and published by Odhams

Newspapers   The Daily Herald

Reynolds News

The (Sunday) People

Magazines   John Bull

Illustrated

Woman (and Woman & Home,

Woman's Realm etc.)

Mickey Mouse

Eagle Comics (and sister

publications)

Picturegoer (and annual)

Modern Transport

- also responsible for publishing

and printing a number of others

including trade journals

CPSIA information can be obtained
at www.ICGtesting.com
Printed in the USA
LVHW021752291119
638856LV00014B/1021